SALVATION
IN THE
KILLING
FIELDS

AILEEN LUDINGTON AND DARRYL LUDINGTON

Pacific Press Publishing Association
Boise, Idaho
Oshawa, Ontario, Canada

Appreciation to:
Mr. Panno Dok, for his original manuscript, which inspired this book.

Mrs. Aileen Ludington Arthur, for her considerable help in writing, research, and editing.

Edited by Glen Robinson
Designed by Dennis Ferree
Cover by Lynn Bernasconi
Typeset in 10/12 Bookman

Library of Congress Catalog Card Number: 89-63083

ISBN 0-8163-0890-X

91 92 93 94 95 • 5 4 3 2 1

Contents

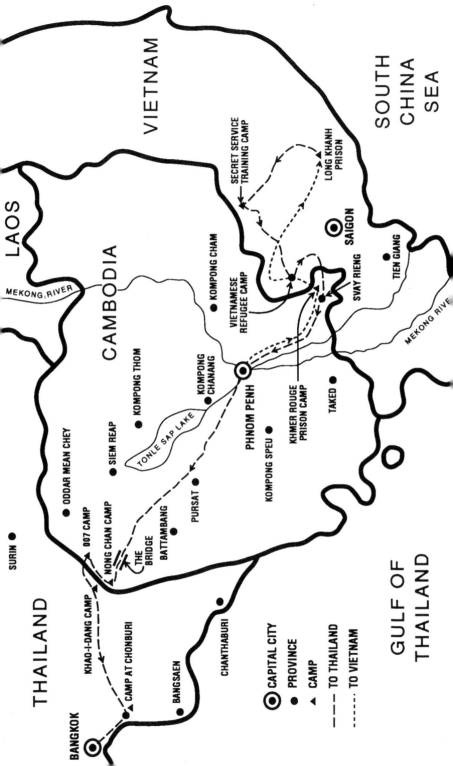

The line between good and evil, hope and despair, does not divide the world between "us" and "them." It runs down the middle of every one of us.

Robert Fulghum

Chapter 1
The Bridge

The bridge! The final barrier to freedom!

Chanla's chest burned with anticipation and fear. Too much depended on such a small obstacle as this bridge.

He looked around carefully, weighing his options. Three armed Vietnamese soldiers stood at the entrance to the bridge. It was not quite 5:00 a.m., and already a long line of people were waiting. The Thai-Cambodian border was just beyond the next village.

Getting over this bridge meant—*freedom!*

It was getting harder for Chanla to understand that word. The simple Cambodian way of life without the pressures of industry and technology had provided plenty of happiness and security for as long as he could remember. To him, *freedom* was just a fancy word used by revolutionaries who wished to change the established ways of life. The French, Lon Nol, the Khmer Rouge, Pol Pot, and now the North Vietnamese; each promised a freedom better than the last.

Chanla wondered where those waiting at the bridge were headed. Wasn't it rather obvious that everyone wanted to escape to the border? How could he convince the soldiers at the checkpoint to allow him and his friends to pass? What convincing reason could he possibly give?

After watching the activity on the bridge for a few minutes, Chanla saw that hardly anyone was getting through. A rooster crowed ominously in the distance.

"Now what are we going to do?" The disheartened words came from one of his friends.

"Doesn't look very hopeful, does it?" said the other.

Chanla himself was deeply troubled as he turned to face his two friends. Their situation looked impossible. But there was no choice. They had to go on, at least *he* did. He was a fugitive from the Vietnamese Secret Police! To go back meant capture, certain torture—even death.

He looked toward the bridge again, wondering if death might be the only real freedom. His throat tightened as he thought of his family in Phnom Penh.

Freedom! Whatever it was, he must find it, at any cost.

A few hours earlier, Chanla and his companions had been riding a truck on the last leg of their journey from Phnom Penh to the northwestern province of Battambang, near the Thai border. Because of Chanla's high position in the new Vietnamese-Cambodian occupation government, he'd had no trouble getting permission to make the trip. His rank and special services uniform brought respectful salutes at checkpoints along the way. Even his two friends were waved through without the usual careful search.

When the battered GMC truck screeched to a halt a few kilometers short of the village, the three men paid the driver and got out.

"Well, Chanla, your permit got us this far," Pran said as they walked along the road. "But it's not going to get us to the border."

Bunna sighed. "I don't know a single person in this province. I'm not even sure where we are!"

The future looked bleak for the three friends. They had started out confidently from Phnom Penh with what seemed like a good plan, but now they felt confused. None of them had been this far west, and they were unfamiliar with the region.

"Let's hail a taxi and ask to be driven to the border," Pran suggested. Outgoing and optimistic, sometimes a bit foolhardy, always full of ideas—that was Pran.

Chanla chuckled at the boldness of such a move, but he sobered quickly. "Too obvious. The driver might be a spy, a government sympathizer, or just a Cambodian farmer wanting to impress the authorities. We could quickly be dead men." Chanla's training had made him cautious.

Chanla was also a Christian. Five years before, he had given his heart to a God he believed loved him. During the subsequent years of trial and terror, he had learned to trust that God. Chanla earnestly prayed for direction.

As they discussed their limited alternatives, the taxi idea seemed best after all. They would have to take a chance. The three of them could overpower a driver who acted suspiciously. And Chanla still carried his service pistol.

Breathing a silent prayer, Chanla signaled the next motorcycle taxi that came along. "Drive us to the border," he said pleasantly, pressing a gold coin into the man's hand.

Obviously startled by their request, the driver looked at them carefully. Tension mounted. Chanla fingered his gun as the three began to back away, ready to bolt.

The driver noted their youthful Cambodian faces—faces that mirrored eager hope mingled with the fear, pain, and despair that had marked their lives for so long.

"Wait, wait!" he shouted. Then, speaking in a friendlier tone, he said, "You can't go to the border like that. You wouldn't have a chance." The young men stopped and stared.

"Look, I'll help you. Let me take you to my house. You'll need different clothes, and you'll need papers." He pressed the starter, and the engine roared to life. Hesitantly, they climbed in.

Could they trust this man? Were they bound for safety, or would the next stop be military police headquarters? Each man was silent, intent on his own thoughts. Only Chanla relaxed.

"Thank you, God," he breathed. "I *must* believe, *must* trust that You've brought this man to help us."

When they reached the driver's home at the edge of the village, Chanla received a crude black shirt and a black pair of pants, the common dress of the country people. Chanla had mixed feelings as he exchanged his army uniform for the peasant clothing. That uniform had been his ticket to the elite circles of his occupied country, but now its usefulness was over.

As Chanla emptied his uniform pockets, he looked at his pistol. Should he leave it? It was so small, it would easily fit into his hand. He hesitated a moment, then slipped it into a side pocket of his shoulder bag. He also hid a few gold coins. He pocketed the rest of the money and filled the remaining space in his bag with rice.

Chanla looked over at Bunna, who was busy dismantling his AK-47 Russian-made automatic rifle. Bunna buried the various pieces in his bag of rice.

"If we're searched," Chanla told him, "they'll find that rifle easily. We'd be captured for sure."

"Well, I've seen too many defenseless people tied up and clubbed to death or shot, like dogs, lying helplessly on the ground. If I have to go, I want to go out shooting." Bunna jerked his bag closed.

Chanla dropped the subject but could not shake his sense of foreboding. Was this part of God's plan? Something in the Bible came to mind, about fighting and dying by the gun, or was it the sword?

The taxi driver burned Chanla's uniform and furnished the three with counterfeit papers. He explained that while the border was only thirty-five kilometers (twenty-two miles) away, he could not drive them directly there. They could only request permission to proceed to the next village. When they reached that village, they must then request a permit for the next one along the way.

In this hopscotch fashion, they were able to cover the ten kilometers to the main border village of Sri Ambel by nightfall. At that point, their host bade them farewell. They thanked him warmly and watched him disappear in the distance. Once more they faced the unknown. This was the last village before the big checkpoint near the border. Freedom had never been so close, yet it still seemed far away. They were tired, and very hungry. It was too dark to proceed further without assistance.

As they walked through the village, Chanla prayed again for direction. Whom could they trust? he wondered. He noticed a friendly-looking old man sitting on his doorstep and felt impressed to approach him. *Sompeahing* politely, with bowed head and with his two hands together in the traditional Cambodian manner, Chanla requested food and lodging for the night. The man rose without a word and ushered them into his home. After a simple but welcome meal, their host provided them with a space to sleep.

As he lay on his mat, Chanla thought about the remarkable kindness the village people had shown them along the way. Love filled his heart for his fellow citizens, descendants of the renowned Angkor Wat empire, and for his once-proud country. These thoughts comforted him as he drifted off to sleep.

B-O-O-M!

The explosion shook the house. Chanla jumped up, grabbing a post. From experience he knew that the bomb had been very close. A woman was screaming, and he could make out the dark figures of two soldiers approaching.

After searching the house, the soldiers confronted the old man.

"What are these strangers doing here?" They waved their rifles in the direction of the three young men.

"They are not strangers, comrade," the old man responded quickly, "but friends of mine from the next village, farmers, who have come here for supplies."

The soldiers hesitated, not quite believing the story. But a shout came from the next house, and they hurried out. Chanla knew they'd be back soon, however, if they didn't find the culprits elsewhere.

"Let's get out of here," said Bunna, already assembling his rifle.

Chanla asked their host if he would help them leave the village. The old man hesitated and then went to consult his wife. Nervous over the delay, Chanla placed money on his mat, and the three left noiselessly. In the darkness and confusion, Chanla and his friends were able to slip out of the village and into the countryside unnoticed.

About half an hour later, they heard noises coming down the road behind them. There was no place to hide in the open country with a full moon shining brightly, so they stepped to the side of the road and waited.

An oxcart rattled up alongside them and stopped. The old man, their host from the village, greeted them and motioned them aboard. Relieved, they climbed into the cart and proceeded down the pothole-riddled road. They traveled steadily from 11:00 p.m. until four the next morning, when the old man finally stopped. He told them the bridge was about 150 meters ahead. He urged them to be careful, explaining that the land on either side of the checkpoint was heavily mined. They thanked him and picked up their bags. Once more, Chanla was impressed with the courage and loyalty of the country people. Those in need were quietly helped, no questions asked, no bargains struck.

Despite the early hour, a long line had already formed at the bridge. As the young men mingled with the waiting groups, they learned that they would need permits to get past this point. Few of the people in line had proper papers, but they would nevertheless wait long hours. When their turn came, they would plead with the guards or try to bribe them. Walking closer, Chanla observed that all three guards were Vietnamese. He also observed that nearly everyone trying to get through was turned back.

"You stupid idiots," the guards shouted arrogantly. "We ought to shoot all of you!" The frightened peasants, not understanding the language but comprehending the rejection, turned back with heavy hearts.

The three men withdrew to the nearby forest, squatting in a circle to talk over their situation. Chanla observed that the Vietnamese guards did not speak Cambodian, and no one was translating for them. A legal permit was the only thing the soldiers recognized. Persons crossing the border either produced one, or were crudely threatened and driven back.

All three friends spoke Vietnamese. Chanla and Bunna had been imprisoned by the Vietnamese, and because of their knowledge of French, had served as translators and later as army officers. Both were now deserters. Pran had grown up in a village along the Vietnamese border. After considerable discussion, it was decided that Chanla and Bunna would play the part of simple peasants who spoke only Cambodian, and Pran would act as interpreter for them. Pran was better with the language. Besides, if suspicion developed, it would center on Pran, who was less vulnerable than the other two.

Chanla ran his fingers through his short-cropped black hair. His training with the Vietnamese secret service had taught him many ingenious tricks for dealing with the enemy. They needed two things: a good reason for going to the next village, and a diversion; something that would distract the soldiers' attention. Again Chanla pleaded with his heavenly Father.

When they returned to the road a few minutes later, Chanla spotted a young peasant boy carrying a cage. He called him over, and when the boy removed the cover from the cage, they saw that he was carrying two live rabbits. The three friends looked at each other, chuckling at the turn of events.

"Sell us your rabbits," Bunna said, holding out a tempting sum of money.

Noting their interest, the boy countered with a higher price. After some bartering, the exchange was made.

The young men were soon walking down the road, laughing and talking to each other in Cambodian, trying to appear as natural as possible. The next moments would be crucial, one way or the other.

Continuing their air of nonchalance, they walked past the line of people and approached the bridge. The sun was up, and the mist was melting away. The countryside took on a warmth and beauty in contrast to the situation ahead. The men could think only of the obstacle that lay between them and the freedom they so desperately sought.

Stepping boldly to the head of the line, Pran surprised the guards by greeting them in Vietnamese, and the guards were visibly pleased to be addressed in their own language. Pran went on to explain his background, mentioning a village in Vietnam he had visited frequently.

"That's my home village!" exclaimed one of the soldiers, stepping closer to Pran.

As the two talked, Chanla slid the cover off the cage. Noticing the rabbits, the other guards walked over and stuck their fingers through the wire and began playing with the furry little creatures.

Pran produced their fake papers and explained that he and his friends were on their way to a big feast in the next village, in honor of his great-uncle's eightieth birthday. A banquet was scheduled, and they were bringing the rice and the rabbits. Naturally friendly, Pran kept up a steady stream of conversation.

"You may go," the guard finally told Pran, "but not your friends."

Chanla's heart sank, though he kept his face carefully blank and uncomprehending. Would Pran be tempted to go on without them? "Give him courage, God," he prayed.

Pran leaned toward the guard in indignation. "What?" he roared. "How can I carry all these supplies by myself?" He indicated the three heavy bags. Then, in a more reasoning tone he said, "You don't have to worry about these farmer boys. They must be back tomorrow to help with the planting."

"The boys" smiled shyly and looked at the ground. Obviously they didn't know what was going on. The guard was enjoying himself. Emboldened by his power over them and flattered by their deference, he waved them through. Shouldering their bags, the men moved quickly. The other guards rose to protest. They were supposed to search each piece of baggage that went past their checkpoint.

But the men were nearly across the bridge. The guards shrugged and turned to the next group in line.

Chanla's heart was pounding! A miracle—in fact, a *double* miracle! Ruthless guards, specially trained to pick out would-be escapees, had allowed them to walk right through. And had forgotten to check their baggage!

Chanla knew this was the last official checkpoint. Ahead lay several kilometers of no-man's land along the borders of Cambodia and Thailand. Directly ahead was a large clearing, with no trees, shrubs, or water. This open area discouraged any heroic attempts to sprint past the checkpoint. A fleeing man would be an easy target.

As Chanla and his friends traversed the clearing, they approached three more soldiers beside the roadway. The first, holding a rifle, quietly observed them. The soldier next to him held a mine detector and walked along with his head down, studying the ground. The third soldier was lighting a cigarette. Chanla felt a rush of fear as he remembered his carefully hidden pistol. Would the metal detector pick that up? And even if he were able to pass, how about Bunna, behind him, with his large rifle hidden in his rice?

Pran walked past without incident. As Chanla approached, the soldier with the mine detector stopped. He glanced up at Chanla, then looked back at the ground.

"What's the matter?" the first soldier asked his comrade. "Why did you stop?"

The second soldier again looked at Chanla, and back to the ground. "Look at those boots," he said in Vietnamese. "This man is wearing Vietnamese army boots!"

Chanla felt his body turn to ice as the three soldiers surrounded him. How could he have overlooked the boots? He dropped his head, a condemned man, but his heart rose heavenward.

"Please, God," he pleaded, his eyes closing in desperation. "One more miracle. *Just one more miracle!*"

Chapter 2
The Exodus

Chanla couldn't remember a time when his country had been at peace. He grew up in a small province in eastern Cambodia near Vietnam's frontier. If there were no internal conflicts, there was always trouble with the Vietnamese, who believed that both Cambodia and Laos were part of their ancient homeland. They were unrelenting in their efforts to reclaim it.

Border problems became progressively worse in 1969. Vietnamese troops began building camps on Cambodian soil, claiming to be only "borrowing" the land in order to rest between battles. Invasions, sabotage, and terrorist activities increased. Criminals and thieves multiplied. The central government was increasingly unsuccessful in controlling the situation. Along the borders, political corruption was rampant.

In 1970, while Cambodia's Prince Norodom Sihanouk was out of the country, his Royalist government was overthrown. Lt. General Lon Nol came to power and formed the New Republic Regime. The new government promised greater freedom to the people and more determined resistance to Communism.

These changes did little to help the villages outside of the protective influence of Phnom Penh. Schools were blown up, rice fields destroyed, and poverty increased. In 1972 Chanla's father obtained work in Phnom Penh and moved his family to the relative safety of the capital city.

17

Despite the border turmoil, a mood of peace and prosperity surrounded the capital. Lon Nol's Republic regime was popular there. By 1975 the raging civil war in Vietnam was winding down. Hope grew for a truce on the borders.

Dok Savang (Dok, the surname, is placed first in Cambodian) wakened his two elder sons early each morning. Chanla and Panno resented having to get up an hour before the rest of the family, but they dared not complain. Dok Savang was the classic oriental father, a stern disciplinarian. The family obeyed him in fear and awe, though Mother called him Baang (dear) and always smiled a special little smile, no matter how upset he seemed to be. She had married him at age sixteen, and borne him four sons and four daughters.

They had no servants, so the couple taught the children to share in the work of the home. Grandma, Mother, and the girls did the marketing and cooking, while Father and sons took care of the housecleaning and chores. During this early morning hour, the boys helped their father draw water for the day, and then they scrubbed the floors.

"My sons must be responsible and hard-working," he told them over and over. Also, he said, "Men must take care of the women."

Father taught in a nearby school, and all the children who were old enough attended.

Although Chanla never admitted it out loud, he had a hard time liking his father. Father was too stern, too serious, too worried about politics, and he continually lectured them on the value of an education. If they were to escape a lifetime of rice farming, he would explain again and again, they must go to school. And they must set a good example. *Always* set a good example! "There is a time for work and a time for play," he would say, "but you must follow the rules." "The rules," it seemed to the boys, allowed precious little time for play.

When Chanla became a Christian, Father was visibly upset. "How dare you bring the foreigners' religion into our home!" he raged. "We've had our own way of worship for generations. It's part of our heritage, our culture."

Chanla keenly felt his father's wrath, but would not argue with him.

"You have parents to teach you right from wrong," he lectured sternly. "You are only seventeen. How can you possibly know what you should believe?" The battle continued for days.

Mother's heart ached for Chanla. She hugged her son and told him privately that she would respect his decision. A year younger, his brother Panno also accepted his decision, although he didn't really understand it.

Chanla hadn't planned on becoming a Christian. It began innocently enough the day he saw a sign advertising free English Bible lessons. He didn't care what textbook they used; his aim was to learn English. Father was glad to see his eldest son making good use of his time. An outstanding student, Chanla could easily cope with a few more classes. What Father didn't realize was that his son would also learn about Christianity.

Chanla began studying "The Good News of Matthew," followed by "The Good News of Mark, Luke, and John." He became totally engrossed in these lessons. The concept of a supreme God to whom he could personally pray intrigued him. He felt great joy in learning about Jesus, his Elder Brother and Saviour.

Chanla sensed Father wouldn't approve. At first Chanla studied the Bible only at school or in the Bible classes. He prayed silently under his mosquito net. He spent as much time with his Christian friends as he dared without arousing suspicion. But as the weeks progressed, Chanla felt convicted that he should take his stand and be baptized.

Father was devastated. He had never before been challenged by a family member! Day after day he agonized over what he perceived as betrayal.

"You are my eldest son. You are to follow me as the family leader. You must be a good example. How can you do this thing?" The air was heavy with tension, and no one had much to say at mealtimes.

Weary of the constant strife, Chanla retreated to the church. One night, soon after he arrived, his brother Panno came with a message that he was wanted at home.

Feeling the need of support and comfort from his friends, he refused to go. It was very late when he finally slipped through the door of his home.

Father was waiting. He directed his son to the backyard. Chanla had never seen his father so angry. Although Father was not a violent man, Chanla steeled himself for the beating he was sure would come.

Father paced about, struggling for control. At length he stopped, and the two faced each other.

"My son," Father began, "in your whole life you have never disobeyed me." His voice was heavy with sorrow and pain. "In every way you have been a son to be proud of." Father looked away, not wanting to betray the emotions he was feeling.

He went on. "As you know, I've been upset about your interest in Christianity. I see it as a threat to our traditions, our way of life." Father paused again.

"But what happened tonight was worse than that. You openly disobeyed me. If that is what your new religion teaches, you must make a choice. I cannot tolerate such behavior in this household."

If Father had beaten him, Chanla could not have felt worse. He groped for words.

"Father, you are right. I have done a terrible thing, and I am very, very sorry. It will never happen again."

Chanla paused and then continued. "My new religion teaches that children must honor and respect their parents. I have sinned against my God and my family."

Chanla sounded so miserable that Father's attitude softened. Finally he spoke again.

"Chanla, I will respect your religion. You may go to your church. But if there is an emergency, if I send for you, come to me immediately. You must not neglect your family responsibilities."

Chanla's cheeks were wet. "Thank you, Father," he said quietly as he bowed his head. He withdrew to his bedroom. Sometime toward morning, Father retired also.

At the evening meal, the Dok family usually took time to discuss the day's happenings. Predictably, Father would voice his increasing concerns for the country. The fighting in the villages was getting worse. Atrocities occurred more frequently, and jobs were increasingly scarce. So little food and medicine were available that people were dying. Villagers were losing confidence in the government and were taking power into their own hands.

But Father's warnings were lost on his family. They had prospered during their three years in the city. Father was a community leader with a secure and respected job. The family had plenty to eat, and they lived in pleasant, middle-class comfort. Father had even purchased five choice pieces of land near the airport, one for himself, and one for each of his sons for their future families. He also owned a motorcycle and two bicycles. His children were aware of unrest and occasional uprisings in the city, but in their young minds, life was bright and trouble seemed far away. They wished their father wasn't such a pessimist.

That fateful day of April 17, 1975, came during the Cambodian New Year's Holiday, a three-day celebration during which schools and businesses were closed. Father awakened his sons as usual, and they did their chores. Then they accompanied him outside to work on the motorcycle. Suddenly they heard a low rumble, like distant thunder. Explosions followed, and black smoke rose from the edge of the city. Father rushed inside and turned on the radio, and heard only hissing static.

The family ate breakfast in silence. Father, not sure of what was happening, did not want to prematurely upset them. They all sensed his worry. About 8:00 a.m., the radio static stopped, and a tight-voiced announcer read a prepared statement:

"There has been an attack by American imperialist troops. The military has taken over the protection of the city. Stay in your homes until you receive further instructions."

"What has happened to the Republic regime and to our president, Lon Nol?" Father was clearly alarmed. "I must find out what is going on."

Father ran quickly down the street to the school, but no

one was there. He circulated around the neighborhood, but confusion reigned. Warnings continued about the "American attack," and the people were told to stay indoors and prepare for bombing. No planes appeared, however, though the shelling around the city grew louder and more fierce.

That afternoon an announcer explained that, due to the inability of Lon Nol and the Republic regime to cope with the present crisis, the military had taken over and installed a new government. The people were ordered once again to stay home and wait for instructions. Father told the family he feared the takeover was connected with the Khmer Rouge, the peasant guerilla soldiers they remembered from their village days. Uncertainty and fear enveloped them, and they wondered what to do.

With his usual caution, Father began assembling the family's valuables. Mother and the older boys were sent to gather food, and the children played listlessly. Son Piteak, twelve, too old to play with the children and too young to join his brothers, stayed with his father, running errands and asking questions. The announcer's words continued:

"The military will save the city. They are routing the evil Republic regime which enslaved the poor people. They will repel the American invaders and bring true freedom to our country."

The propaganda has started, thought Father. What will become of us now? After packing their most valuable and essential possessions and tying them into bundles, the family slept fitfully the rest of the night. Mortar fire was heavy in the outskirts, but no bombs fell on the city.

Early the next morning, they heard the rumble of machinery and the sounds of shouting. Tanks and truckloads of soldiers drove along the streets, cheering and waving flags of victory. People ran outside, holding up white flags of surrender. The Dok family joined the others, straining for a glimpse of their conquerors.

Father stiffened at what he saw. His worst fears were realized. The victory flags were red, and the soldiers wore black, pajamalike peasant clothing with red sashes around their heads or waists. The sandals on their feet were made from rubber truck tires. Each also had a machine gun, or a large rifle. The rebellious country people were taking over the city.

The Khmer Rouge were Cambodian Communists who had been indoctrinated, trained, and equipped by North Vietnamese troops camped along their common borders. Primarily peasants and farmers who were poor and uneducated, they had become increasingly alienated from the central government.

As the Khmer Rouge gained in numbers and strength, they took control of increasing amounts of the countryside. When the war in Vietnam ended and the Vietnamese troops returned to rebuild their own country, the Chinese continued to encourage and supply the Khmer Rouge.

Father had lived most of his life in the border province of Svay Rieng. In the early days of the Khmer Rouge movement, he had tried to cooperate with village leaders, hoping for a peaceful solution that would unite the country. But leadership was weak. Soldiers began fighting each other and raiding nearby villages. The people were increasingly disorganized and oppressed. Anxious for the safety of his family as well as for their education, Father had been thankful to escape to the city.

He now looked around at his family. They lived in a roomy, comfortable home. He had a respected job. Their lives had been relatively safe and peaceful for the past three years. Father clenched his fists. "No! No! This cannot be happening—"

New announcements began:

"For the safety of our citizens and the protection of our beautiful city, the new leadership requests that all civilians evacuate immediately. I repeat, immediately! Take enough food and clothes for three days. By that time we will have repelled the American invaders and secured the safety of our city. Plan to leave as soon as possible."

"We must go," Father said grimly. "We must carry as many of our possessions as we can. There is no certainty about coming back." Father looked tired and beaten. Chanla felt a surge of sympathy for him.

"Don't worry, Father," he said impulsively, "God will take care of us!"

Fire rose in Father eyes. "Your God was executed along with other common criminals," he said bitterly. "How can He help us now?"

Chanla was silent. He longed to share his peace and faith with his distressed father. In the year since his baptism, Chanla had experienced much positive growth. Like Daniel, he prayed and read his Bible three times a day. But unlike Daniel, he didn't do it openly. He studied in private and prayed silently. He loved going to church and spent his spare time there. Although Father did not forbid this, he seldom let an opportunity pass to ridicule his son's religion.

"Leave your God out of this family, or you can stay here and die like He did."

Chanla and Panno helped Father load their possessions onto the motorcycle and two bicycles. The rest of the family brought the bundles, and the men tied them securely in place. After loading the bundles, the men pushed the vehicles, making their way to the school, where several other families had gathered. One of Mother's brothers and one of Father's uncles were there, each with his family.

Father and Panno returned to secure their home just as a squadron of black-clad Khmer Rouge arrived. The soldiers ordered them to leave immediately. Flourishing their automatic weapons, the soldiers marched into the house next door. A loud argument could be heard, followed by shots and screams.

"We must leave quickly," Father said as he rejoined the family. "They mean business. They are already shooting those who question their orders."

Father was a capable man, a leader in the family and the neighborhood. The group followed him as they joined the procession streaming out of the city. People were clutching their children and pushing carts, wagons, bicycles, even cars and buses loaded with their possessions. Many old, feeble, and crippled people, as well as pregnant women and small children, struggled along. Sick patients from hospitals were forced to join the massive throng. And every few feet they passed soldiers waving rifles and threatening to shoot anyone who stopped or tried to turn back.

Later they began passing the corpses of those who had died in the battle for the city. Most were civilians, including women and children, who had been caught in the cross-fire, or who had resisted the Khmer Rouge in some way. Many cars and trucks stood abandoned along the road, windows shattered by rifle shots. Chanla looked inside one of them and saw three dead bodies. He was glad his father had not tried to start the motorcycle. He tied his scarf around his nose to filter the smell of death that was already permeating the air. The story of Sodom and Gomorrah came to mind, especially the part about the angels urging Lot and his family to leave before the final destruction. Was this happening again?

By afternoon, soldiers were systematically combing through each home and machine gunning anyone who still remained. Fear and terror kept the procession moving despite hunger, thirst, and fatigue. Unfeeling soldiers heartlessly shot stragglers. There was no relief from the heat and humidity. Grandma grew especially tired, and Mother took her arm and encouraged her. Father placed the two smallest girls atop the bundles on the motorcycle he and Chanla were pushing.

As evening approached, people began stopping, and this time the soldiers did not object. Father tried to organize his group of twenty-seven people, and sent Chanla and Panno to inquire about possible shelter.

Panno ran ahead, while Chanla walked across the street to a movie theater. Seeing no soldiers, he walked through the open door. The place appeared to be deserted. He made his way through the darkness into the main auditorium.

"Hello," he called tentatively. "Is there room for a few more people in here?" His voice died, the silence absolute. He fumbled in his pockets for a matchbook and struck a flame. In its feeble light, he glimpsed a nightmare that would last a lifetime. Around him on all sides, the machine-gunned bodies of innocent men, women and children filled an entire theater.

In that one ghastly moment, Chanla grasped the reality of the revolution. The peaceful Cambodian way of life he had known for eighteen years was gone, forever!

Chapter 3
"There Is No God"

Numb with shock, Chanla quickly left the theater and walked down the road. He felt frightened and alone, despite the surging crowd. He groped for spiritual consolation.

As he walked, he thought about what he had read in the Bible. Jesus, God's own Son, was betrayed, tortured, and murdered at the hands of His countrymen. Yes, Jesus would understand Chanla's situation. And the same God who sustained His Son during that time of trial comforted Chanla now.

In the meantime, Panno returned to the family.

"Father, it's safer for us to remain in the street. Soldiers are threatening those who try to leave the roadway."

Mother noted a flash of pride in Father's eyes as their newly grown-up second son gave his report. He then turned to stake out space for the family on the pavement. Mother and Grandma rummaged through the food baskets.

Eventually Chanla returned, quietly stepping into place around the makeshift meal. Everyone was tired, but he noticed that his father was especially quiet and withdrawn. Father had always been able to care for his family. They had never gone hungry. They had never slept on the street! Chanla tried to imagine how this proud man felt as he stood by, helpless now. Although Father was outwardly calm, Chanla knew that within he was churning with rage, fear, and frustration, and his son's tender heart ached for him.

27

The night hours passed slowly. Shouts and bursts of gunfire frequently punctuated the darkness, but fatigue and excitement had taken their toll. Even the adults dozed part of the time.

At dawn the soldiers ordered everyone to get moving and prodded the slower ones with their rifle butts. Grabbing some food, the family secured their things and rejoined the procession. Chanla and Father pushed the motorcycle. Panno and Prok, his nine-year-old brother, pushed one bicycle and Piteak, nearly thirteen, wheeled the second one with his eleven-year-old sister, Pitura. Mother took turns helping them and looking after Grandma and the younger children.

For a while the small girls played tag, dodging and dancing about, engrossed in their games. When they tired, Father put two-year-old Chande and Vivatny, four, back atop the vehicles. Seven-year-old Reni chose to walk with the others. Fragile little Grandma surprised everyone by talking optimistically and not complaining at all.

The street was heavily congested, and by noon the group had covered only a kilometer (0.6 mile). Hot, tired, hungry, and blistered, they were glad when Father called them to stop at the side of the road. Mother was holding a pot of rice when a soldier approached.

"You can't stop here," he shouted. "You must keep moving."

"We've been walking for six hours," Father explained patiently. "Grandma and the small girls must have some food and a few moment's rest."

"It's not allowed," the soldier yelled. "No one can stop." He walked over and knocked the rice pot out of Mother's hand, waving his gun menacingly in their faces.

The family moved quickly. When Pitura started to retrieve the rice pot, Mother grabbed the girl's shoulder firmly. Even the little ones were solemn now. No one talked. Bone weary and frightened, they moved along numbly, as in a nightmare.

Chanla realized that the city had virtually shut down. Stores were closed and markets deserted. The usual bustle and noise were replaced by an eerie silence, punctuated only by tramping feet and occasional machine-gun fire. All semblance of friendliness and courtesy among the people disappeared. They were experiencing a stark battle for survival. Chanla thought about his Christian friends. He asked God to be with them and to guide his own family to safety. Despite the confusion around him, he felt peace in his heart.

By evening they reached the suburbs. Father obtained permission to occupy an abandoned house, and his party of twenty-seven men, women, and children crowded into the two small rooms. Supper was especially appreciated, but Mother worried about their dwindling food supplies.

Chanla and his brother Piteak walked down to the river to cool their aching bodies and to bring back water for the others. In the gathering darkness, they saw large objects floating by, some black and some brightly colored. Using a branch, Piteak maneuvered one of them closer. To their horror, it was the body of a young woman, obviously pregnant. She had been stabbed repeatedly, and her body was beginning to bloat.

Both boys felt sick. What kind of army was this? Soldiers were not known for their patience, but these ignorant peasant revolutionaries apparently lacked even the most basic morality and compassion. Chanla and Piteak watched other corpses float by until they could stand it no longer.

Back at the house, family members were clearing out niches and preparing for the night. The children roamed about, nervous and tearful. Noting that his father had gone to the river, Chanla gathered the children for a story. He told them about Jonah and the whale, and how God turned a bad situation into a good one.

"Can your God really do that?" seven-year-old Reni asked, eyes round and earnest. Chanla took his little sister in his arms and hugged her.

"Yes, God can do anything. He will take care of us and help Father make the right decisions."

Father returned in time to hear this last remark, but went straight to his sleeping mat. There was no outburst, no reaction, no fire in his eyes. As Chanla tried to sleep that night, he pondered the change. His father's silence worried him more than the ridicule he'd come to expect.

The house was crowded and hot. The younger boys, Piteak and Prok, secured permission to sleep behind the house and carried out their mats and blankets. All was well until daylight; then they rushed in, pale and frightened.

"There's a dead body out there!" Piteak choked out. "We were sleeping right beside it."

"It's a policeman," added Prok, his eyes large as saucers. "He's got his uniform on."

"What if they blame it on us?" Piteak was old enough to worry.

Father went out to investigate. The man had been dead for a couple of days, probably killed during the battle for the city. Father didn't think there would be trouble.

The third day of the exodus was the worst. Movement was at a snail's pace. The farther they walked, the more horror unfolded. Human bodies littered the landscape, some hanging out of cars and buildings, others blocking their progress on the street. Sometimes they were kicked aside, but no one attempted to bury them. Most were bloated and decomposing. Breathing was difficult. People tied pieces of cloth over their noses and mouths in an attempt to cut out the stench.

At every junction and turn, black-pajama-clad soldiers with Chinese revolutionary-style caps stood fingering the triggers of their rifles. The Khmer Rouge recruited boys fifteen years and older, but some of the soldiers seemed scarcely that old. Armed with powerful AK-47 automatic rifles, they strutted about importantly. They continually threatened, and frequently fired at anyone who argued, fell behind, or otherwise annoyed them.

By late afternoon, the refugees reached the city limits and fanned out into the countryside. That night the family camped in the open, across from a temple. Mother sent the older boys to a nearby village to look for food. Panno circled the town in one direction, and Chanla the other, but no one wanted to sell what they had.

Chanla found a tree with ripe mangoes. As he reached

to pick one, he heard the metallic click of a gun cocking behind him. He turned to face a young man about his own age. Cambodians are naturally friendly people, and normally these young men would have greeted each other in an amiable manner. But nothing was normal now.

"Halt," ordered the soldier. "This is a people's tree. You are not allowed to touch it. You must get permission."

Chanla bowed, hands together in the courteous Cambodian manner. "Please, sir, my family is traveling to our home village, and we need food. May I gather a few pieces of fruit for our supper?"

There was a long pause as the two men looked at each other. "Don't say *sir*," the soldier said crossly, "and no more *sompeahs*. We are now comrades, brothers." He looked around nervously. "My orders are to guard these trees and shoot anyone trying to pick and sell the fruit. We must rid our country of capitalists who try to make profits by stealing from the common people. You may pick only what you will eat tonight."

Chanla filled his basket and returned to the family. Father looked solemn as his son recounted the experience. He called the group together.

"We must be extremely careful of what we say," Father warned. "There is no way to distinguish enemies from friends. The less we talk, the better." Father paused a few moments, but no one moved.

"The Khmer Rouge are composed mostly of uneducated farmers and country peasants. They fear and distrust city people and have no respect for education. They've been taught that educated people are the ones who have oppressed them." Father fell silent again. The family began to understand their dangerous and precarious situation.

After supper, the family again gathered around Father. They were camped in an open field, with no one else nearby. Father began talking about his youth during the Japanese occupation. He, along with many other peace-loving Cambodian young men, did not want to fight in the war. They learned to live by their wits. They slept in fields, streets, and barns. They worked as peasants, planting rice and tending animals, and they often ate grass and plants to survive. They blended into the countryside, appearing shabby and ignorant. Thus they were able to elude government recruiters until World War II ended.

Chanla looked at his father and tried to imagine this educated, cultured man in such a condition. He and Panno decided their father must be exaggerating, the way he did when he repeatedly told his "lazy sons" how hard he'd had to work as a boy.

After the war, Father had determined to get an education and have a better life. He worked his way through school and eventually became a policeman. He married and started a family. But he continued taking classes, nourishing a dream he had in his heart. In time, he became a qualified teacher.

Father's education commanded a good job, and he worked with zest and industry. As his influence widened in the village and in the province, he became a respected leader, and the family enjoyed many privileges. He continued his thrifty ways, and they lacked for nothing.

"But, look, everything is now lost," Father said bitterly, as they sat in the field, their possessions in a few bundles around them. For a moment, tears seemed close, but the moment passed.

"You've seen ignorant, uneducated peasants come with guns and help themselves to everything we have worked a lifetime for! They herd us out into the pasture like animals! How can such a thing happen to our country? To our people? To us! If I ever entertained the thought that there could be a God, I know now that there is not. We have been left to perish. There is no one to help us. We will be driven to exhaustion. We will all die."

Father was spent. He bowed his head and remained silent. The night was as dark as their future. Long after the others slept, Father sat wrestling with his decision.

Chapter 4
Angka's Country

Hours later, Mother awoke and realized Father was not beside her. She quietly made her way to his side and slid her hand into his.

"Dear wife, I have been laboring over our future." He sighed wearily. "I'm sure no one will be returning to the city. It was merely a plot to get rid of us. We must abandon any hope of returning to our home in Phnom Penh."

Father spoke evenly, with conviction, but Mother sensed his pain and despair. She leaned closer and pressed his hand.

"Yes, Baang, I agree with you. They have no intention of allowing anyone to go back."

Father continued slowly, in measured words. "I have been wrestling with a decision and searching for an acceptable answer. I have decided it would be best to return to our old home village in the Svay Rieng province. But it is a very long journey, almost to the Vietnamese border." He looked at Mother, wanting her reaction. The moon had come up, and he could see her face clearly.

"A good decision," Mother answered thoughtfully. "We are well-known, having left only three years ago. We have many relatives and friends there." She paused, then added, "We have quite a few staples with us. I believe we can purchase enough food along the way to make the trip."

The rest of the family had mixed reactions when they heard the news. The children begged to return to their

33

home and friends in Phnom Penh. Grandma, Chanla, and Panno, however, realized the hopelessness of that solution and were encouraged by the thought of returning to their old home village.

On the sixth day of the exodus, Mother's brother announced that he had found relatives, and his family would stay in the village of Kakai. By the second week, the other family also found a location. But Dok Savang and his family pressed on. They bartered for food and slept in temples, ruins of schools, and abandoned houses, as well as in the open fields and forests.

As they traveled, they witnessed the remains of their once-thriving and prosperous country. Schools, businesses, and government buildings had been bombed, most homes were in ruins, and many farms had been burned. Broken bricks and damaged vehicles were scattered about. They continued to pass swollen, rotting corpses of men, women, and children. The smell of death was everywhere. They held the scarves tightly around their noses.

An unexpected bright spot developed. Day after day, frail, seventy-five-year-old Grandma grew stronger. Some days they were able to walk as far as twenty kilometers (12.4 miles). She not only kept up, but began helping with the cooking and the children. She sang songs of her girlhood and gently joked about their ordeal. Chanla loved to walk beside her, urging her to tell him stories of the past. He felt proud of her, proud of his family, proud of the people who had built this once-beautiful country. And he especially loved this gentle woman, who had been an integral part of their family ever since he could remember.

Father, however, became an increasing concern. Chanla sensed his deepening depression. During the long hours spent pushing the motorcycle, he gradually became quieter and more withdrawn. His shoulders drooped, and he seemed to visibly shrink in size. His remarks were mostly bitter outbursts: "What will become of the family? We are running out of supplies and will be forced to starve! Everything I have worked for in my life is gone—gone forever!" Then he would lapse into long, stony silences.

Four weeks after leaving Phnom Penh, they arrived at

their home village. Guards were redirecting people else-where.

"But this is my hometown, comrade," insisted Father, his voice rising. "I have relatives here. I am well known."

"No city people are allowed in this village unless Angka authorizes it," the soldier answered. "Where are your papers? Unless you have a permit from Angka, you cannot go farther."

Father was speechless with frustration and shock. Chanla spoke up.

"Who is Angka? Where can we find him?"

"You cannot come here," the young guard repeated. "Go find a smaller village and learn to work." He spoke with contempt, as though to slow-witted children. "And learn about Angka. Angka is the new party. Angka makes the rules now." His impatience was obvious. He was tired of city refugees.

"What shall we do, Father?" Panno asked when they could not be overheard. Panno was seventeen, a high-school senior who had planned to become a lawyer. The past few weeks had toughened his muscles, developed his backbone, and given him a new sense of responsibility. "We can't go back to the city. We must find another village."

They waited patiently as Father stared at the ground in silence. His last hope had been crushed. His desire to return to the village of his youth, the place where he had raised his family, was not to be. He could scarcely absorb this disappointment.

"What about the village where you were born?" Mother asked tentatively. "Your sister's family is still there. Per-haps they would help us."

"We will go," Father decided. "It is a small village. I don't think this—*Angka*—will bother us there."

As they walked along the road again, Chanla thought about Abraham, moving his family at God's direction to an unknown destination. He prayed that God would guide and care for them as He had for Abraham.

A week later, the family arrived in the village of Toul Ta Yuan. Chanla's uncle and aunt invited them into their home, and everyone was glad to stop. Mother and Grandmother went to the kitchen with the women, while Father and the boys unpacked necessities for the night.

News quickly circulated that Dok Savang and his family had arrived. Father was well known in the region, and people began calling on him. For a time, talking with old friends, former students, and relatives, Father seemed restored. A village official dropped by and talked with Uncle.

At supper that evening, the family recounted their long trip from Phnom Penh. Uncle and Aunt listened quietly; too quietly, Chanla thought. Finally, Uncle rose to speak.

"I'm glad to welcome my honorable brother-in-law and his family to our humble home. You may rest here and refresh yourselves." He smiled briefly, then spoke again. "This small and friendly village has been our home for many years. Recently we've had a great influx of refugees. Each day, more city people are arriving, and our village leaders are working hard to find places for them." He seemed nervous and uneasy. He sipped a drink, set it down, and continued.

"As you know, we have a new government now, called Angka. This regime is dedicated to freeing our people from the control of greedy foreign imperialists and government bureaucrats. To ensure the success of this effort, we, the people, are asked to delete the past from our minds, and not to talk of it or think of it again. We must talk only of the future, of Angka's plans for us. Angka will solve our problems, leading us to a better life and to true freedom."

Uncle took a long breath and sipped his drink again. "Tomorrow morning, village officials will escort you to orientation meetings in the courtyard of the temple. You are expected to take your things and go with them."

Shocked, Chanla and Panno looked at each other in disbelief. They would not be able to stay with their uncle. And worse, he sounded like a Communist! Had he surrendered so quickly?

They turned toward Father. Surely he would bring Uncle to his senses. Father would know better than to be deceived by such outrageous lies.

But their father thanked Uncle and assured him they

would cooperate fully. He motioned his elder sons to follow him. When they were out of earshot, Panno exploded.

"Father, how could you sit there and say nothing?" Anger and disgust flowed with the words. "This—this Angka is robbing us of our freedom and murdering our people. It's ruining our country. . . ."

"Seal your mouth, impulsive one," Father commanded. "You will not speak such thoughts again."

Panno's face flushed. He looked at his brother. Chanla was upset too.

"But, Father, we can't just wipe out our whole past, our whole culture." Chanla's voice broke. Father looked down, then straightened as he faced his sons.

"We can if we must." Father's face was grim, with no trace of emotion. "These are new times, and we are ruled by new people. We must cooperate or perish. You are young. It will be harder for the older ones. Quickly adjust to what has happened and help me protect the women and children."

Father's voice was steady, but Chanla and Panno knew he was near the breaking point. The only life he cared about was rapidly fading. The disappointment was crushing him.

"You are my eldest sons," he continued quietly. "I have taught you to work. I have trained you to be responsible and honest. You are well educated. I have cared for this family for nearly twenty years. It may soon be your turn.

"If anything happens to me, you must be responsible for the others." He put his hands on his sons' shoulders. "I've been a very strict father, and I've been hard on you. But I felt it was necessary. I wanted you to be strong men— leaders—good examples. Don't be angry with me if I've been too harsh."

Father looked at the ground, then back at his sons. His voice softened, and a touch of pride appeared in his eyes. "But all is not lost if my sons are good men."

He could say no more. Chanla and Panno were too deeply moved to speak. They embraced their father, wondering how they had ever imagined him to be hateful and cruel. Tears flowed down Chanla's face.

"You can depend on me, Father. I will live as you taught me. I will take care of our family." Panno assured him likewise.

But Chanla had more on his mind. He spoke with great sincerity. "Father, I pray that you will put your trust in the true God. He can be with you, whatever happens. And He will take care of the rest of us." Chanla's faith was so much an integral part of his thinking that even now he was driven to speak of it.

For once, his father seemed to listen to his words. He looked into Chanla's eyes and saw a young man as stubborn and determined as he was himself, but with an unshakable faith. "Yes, Chanla," he said gently. "If there is a God, He would not forsake a son like you." They walked back to the house in silence.

The Local Action Team arrived early the next morning to escort the entire family to the nearby temple compound. The temple was filled with many other displaced persons. The Dok family were assigned a few feet of floor space, where they placed their possessions. Father and the boys tied the bundles together, and Mother spread a blanket over them. As they left for orientation meetings, they wondered if their things would be searched, or worse yet, stolen.

The children were separated and taken to a special area. They were indoctrinated with pictures and stories and otherwise cared for while the adults reluctantly attended their classes.

Meetings lasted until nightfall and continued for three days. New ways of thinking and living were introduced. Much time was spent detailing the evils of the former Republic regime and explaining how Angka would right the existing wrongs and lead the country to a brilliant future. The people were instructed to close their minds to the past and to think about what was ahead. They were told to develop new thoughts, new attitudes, new convictions. These changes, they were assured, would bring a more complete freedom than they had previously known.

"Buddha is dead. God is dead. There is no god now but

Angka. Angka will provide everything you need. Angka is powerful and wise. Angka is your hope for the future." Father told the boys that Angka was the new government's version of Communist ideology.

Chanla noted that most of the others were displaced city people like themselves. Everyone felt frightened, unsure of what to expect. Even Chanla's genial nature and natural friendliness drew little response. People had grown afraid to talk to each other. And because of crowding and lack of privacy, Chanla soon realized his own family had little they could say to each other.

After supper that night, while the women and children arranged the sleeping areas, the men and older boys were taken for interrogation. It was brisk and businesslike. They were questioned far into the night about their education, jobs, and previous residences. The interrogators also asked for details of their families, relatives, friends, and acquaintances.

Chanla noticed some of the people turning pale and hesitating with their answers. No one knew what consequences their information would bring. Father, Chanla, and Panno told the truth. That was the code the family had lived by, and they did not forsake it now.

On the third day the announcement came that all men over fifteen years of age would report for work detail the next morning. No other information was given. No further interrogation was held that evening.

Chanla slept fitfully. Over the heat and crowding he felt a heavy foreboding, dreaming of bloated bodies, machine guns, and cries of terror. He awoke at dawn, drenched with sweat. After breakfast he hugged his mother, grandmother, sisters, and younger brothers. They said little. He wondered how they felt, but no one felt free to talk.

"I had a disturbing dream," Chanla quietly told Father. "It has given me a sense of dread, a feeling of impending doom."

"I feel it too," Father confessed. "We are losing control over our lives." His voice held an edge of desperation.

Panno was quiet, but he, too, was filled with fear and uncertainty.

Father looked at his sons standing on each side of him. They were competent and reliable, the pride of his life.

"I have confidence in you both," he said in his familiar, serious way. "Whatever happens, be truthful. Keep your dignity. Remember your roots. Don't make trouble. Quietly accept what comes to you." It was Father's creed, and in the days that followed it would be their creed as well.

People milled about expectantly. Some tried to set up crude partitions for their families. Chanla went to check their vehicles, which had been placed in a storage area. About 11:00 a.m. the call came. Swallowing some food Mother had prepared from their supplies, Savang and his sons followed the village sheriff.

Chanla looked back. "Take care of the women," he shouted to Piteak and Prok. At twelve and nine years of age, they were the only "men" left.

At the edge of the village the sheriff picked up a bicycle. As he pedaled, the group ran along behind. But they could not maintain the pace, so they slowed to a brisk walk, interspersed by short runs. When the sheriff got too far ahead, he would stop until they caught up. Periodically they came upon guards who examined their papers and waved them on to the next checkpoint.

Though hours went by, the men received no rest. As soon as they caught up with the sheriff, he would start off again. Chanla began to worry about the increasing distance. He had thought they would work on surrounding farms and return to their families in the evening. He had nothing with him except the clothes on his back.

Occasionally the sheriff would pedal far ahead, and when they caught up they would find him enjoying refreshments at a wayside stand. But the men received nothing. Hunger increased, and thirst became acute. By late afternoon, Chanla's strength was ebbing, and he worried about Father. He prayed silently for strength.

By evening, the group arrived at a large detention center. Several hundred men were already inside, and Chanla spotted a great-uncle and one of his cousins. The sheriff ordered them to wait outside, however, until he could find out where they were to go. The men looked longingly at the people eating and drinking inside.

By the time the sheriff returned, the leaders had begun to divide up the people according to occupation. Chanla, Panno, and the cousin were placed with the student-teacher group, while Father and Great-Uncle were assigned to the group of government employees.

The strange foreboding returned as Chanla watched his father's group being marched away. Father might be bruised, but he would not be bowed. Standing tall and walking with firm steps, he did not look back.

Suddenly, love and appreciation flooded his heart. He wondered if he would ever see his father again.

Chapter 5
The New Equality

It took awhile for Mother to recover after Chanla, Panno, and Father were taken by the sheriff. The family gathered around, trying to comfort her.

"Don't cry, Mother. They will be home soon, probably tonight," said eleven-year-old Pitura.

Mother suddenly realized that her children's needs were now as great as her own. She drew a deep breath and struggled for control. She began hugging them.

"Of course, you're right, my daughter. See? They didn't take any clothes or supplies along." She spoke with a confidence she did not feel.

"Attention! Everyone report to your assigned group." The announcement blared over the loudspeakers, and the family separated to their appointed places. That night, when the others went to bed, Mother waited for the return of her husband and sons.

Day after day, Mother, Grandmother, and the children remained at the pagoda, sharing space with others on the crowded floor of the building and attending indoctrination sessions. They heard no word of the men. After a month, the family was pronounced ready to live in the village, and they were assigned a small house with two other families.

"Mother, why did they take our motorcycle and one of our bicycles?" Piteak asked. "Father worked hard to earn those things. They belong to us."

"And they went through our bundles and took some of

43

our clothes and treasures," Pitura added.

"Our new rulers feel that special things should be shared with others," Mother explained, trying not to show the sadness she felt. "Private ownership of such luxuries is 'capitalistic' and 'greedy,' and we must overcome such tendencies. They promised to store them in the community warehouse."

"Well, I'll bet Father will get them back when he returns. He won't let people just help themselves to our belongings. That's plain stealing." Piteak was not yet ready to accept the possibility of not seeing the treasures again.

They awoke the next morning to shouts in the darkness outside the house. Mother opened the door, and soldiers pushed past her, shining flashlights on the sleeping people in the house.

"Get up, your vacation is over. It's time to go to work." They tramped about, prodding startled children and kicking at furnishings.

"What kind of work are we supposed to do in the night?" Mother demanded. She was a shy woman, but her voice was firm and strong.

"Night? It will soon be dawn. Country people, *proper* people, get up early and work for their food." The lead soldier insolently flashed his light in Mother's face. "I suppose you think rice will magically appear on your table, like it did in the city." He paused, his disgust evident. "Well, it doesn't. From now on, you will get up each morning and work for it." He looked about the room. "All of the women must go to the rice fields. We will come back later for the children."

"Wait . . . please! My aged mother is feeble and ill. My smallest girls are two and four years old. Surely you will allow her to care for them." Mother was surprised at her own courage.

The soldiers talked it over and delivered their verdict. "The old woman may stay and care for the small ones. The other children will go to school and care for the village livestock. The rest of you will come with us."

Mother was shaking, but she bowed respectfully. "We will do as you say." She rolled up her mat and reached for her belt.

Pitura and Reni looked at their usually immaculate mother. She had never left home with unkempt hair and rumpled clothes. In fact, she had always dressed the girls as well, and brushed their hair.

Mother and three other women from the house hurried along the dark path to a clearing beside a large rice field where others had gathered. Soldiers handed the women baskets of rice seedlings, which they were to plant.

Mother had never worked in a rice field. In fact, she'd never worked outside the home. Reared in comfortable middle-class surroundings, she married at sixteen. The family always indulged her. Her husband was a good provider, and he and the older boys handled the heavier household chores. But the men were gone, and today she was handed a basket.

Mother watched the country women remove their sandals, gather their skirts into their waistbands, and step into the water. Mother did likewise, bending to her task and working intently.

For hours she planted rice. Her hands grew raw, and her feet ached with cold. She straightened up from time to time to relieve the pain in her back. Finally, about midmorning, the soldiers called them to the landing. They were allowed to rest and were given a bowl of watery rice gruel.

In early afternoon, they were given another break and another bowl of soupy rice. This time they received a small chunk of salt and a few half-spoiled vegetables as well. The day finally ended about six o'clock, and they were allowed to return home.

That evening, an exhausted Mother collapsed on her mat while Grandma prepared the scant cup of rice they were allotted.

Vivatny and little Chande pressed close to tell Mother about their day. Vivatny was quick and clever, and soon learned to take her little sister to the rice fields to play. When no one was looking, she plucked green plants, rolled them up, and slipped them into her blouse. She also caught small minnows in old cans and found a few edible vegetables, which Grandma cooked with their rice.

Piteak, Pitura, Prok, and Reni had a long day also. They attended school for one hour, then were assigned to feed the pigs, clean their pens, and herd the village cattle and water buffalo to nearby pastures. The children each received responsibility for taking care of specific animals. Seven-year-old Reni and nine-year-old Prok adapted easily, running about and playing games as the animals grazed.

But twelve-year-old Piteak worried constantly. He was a serious, conscientious lad and had been told they would be severely punished if an animal became lost or injured, or if it died. He continually checked on his brother and sisters, and helped them if they had trouble. When he was alone out on the hillsides, he sometimes pretended he was Father. He practiced his father's walk and mannerisms and tried to mimic his serious way of talking. It made him feel stronger and braver.

Eleven-year-old Pitura was another story. She was small for her age, with delicate features, and had lived a very sheltered life. She'd never even touched a farm animal. As they neared the pig pens, she drew back, revolted by the stinking, slime-covered creatures.

"What a spoiled city brat!" the guard jeered. "Well, you won't be pampered here. *Move!*"

When she still hesitated, he raised his rifle butt. She quickly waded into the mud, waves of nausea rolling over her.

It was the worst day of Pitura's life. She spent her time doing things she had never, in her worst nightmares, imagined she would do. The swine were dirty, smelly, and contrary. Later, she was sent to the nearby pasture, where she wearily herded, prodded, and chased stubborn, mindless cattle.

When she got home, she threw herself on the mat next to Mother, tears running down her face.

"Just look at these blisters! Every part of my body aches." Mother patted her, trying to comfort her.

". . . and I have to do this every single day—tomorrow, next week, *forever*, probably. The soldiers are so mean— and no one cares. I just can't—!"

"Shush, daughter. Remember what Father said. We are now country people, and we must fit in. We must learn to accept what happens to us."

Mother was having her own problems. Her hands were raw, and her feet were cut and swollen. She'd never felt so tired in her life. How she needed her strong, protective husband!

Now, however, she became the family's strength. After working twelve hours in the rice fields beneath the broiling sun, she came home to bandage wounds, soak sprained muscles, kiss bruises, and soothe aching hearts. She infused fresh courage into tired bodies. She cuddled frightened children and sought to ease Pitura's pain. Her cheerfulness and natural friendliness quickly permeated the neighborhood, and people began to nod and smile at her and to each other.

After the others were asleep, however, Mother's façade fell, and tears flowed unchecked. Her body ached, and the loneliness became unbearable. Where was the husband who'd been at her side for twenty years? Theirs had been a love match from the start. She liked the way Savang looked, the way he walked, the way others looked up to him. He loved her warmth, her sunny disposition, the way she smelled. Despite his stern exterior, he was a gentle, caring husband. She longed to lean on his broad shoulders and share with him the heavy weight she now bore.

Mother worried about her sons too. She missed affectionate, thoughtful Chanla, and Panno's optimistic enthusiasm. She was proud of the young men they'd become. The morning they left with Father, she'd had no hint that they would not return that evening. Rumors circulated about prisons, labor camps, and death squads. She hoped the three were still alive. How long could she bear the uncertainty, the hard labor, the slow starvation, the threats and demands of the soldiers?

Sheer will and determination propelled her. The family must not sense her anguish. By day, she radiated courage and optimism. She talked about Father, Chanla, and Panno. She washed their clothes and folded them in neat piles beside their sleeping mats. She befriended her neighbors and co-workers. Only late at night did she allow reality to overwhelm her. At those times she felt utterly alone. She wished she knew Chanla's God.

As the weeks dragged by, malnutrition took its toll. Their clothes seemed to hang more loosely, and their strength and energy ebbed. They all became more solemn and talked less and less.

Pitura continued to mourn her lost youth. It was no life at all, only stark, wretched existence. She retreated into her mind. She found a little relief by fantasizing elaborate escapes. She would find her father and brothers, and they would flee to a safe place in the forest. There they would rebuild their home and reunite the family.

One day Grandma took down the dingy pink curtains that hung on the windows. When she washed them, the material looked new and bright again. Her skillful hands fashioned new skirts for Pitura and Reni, and new blouses for the two little girls.

"Grandma, how beautiful!" the girls squealed in delight that night. Even Pitura's sad face brightened as they modeled their latest fashions. They put them on the next morning and kissed Grandma. Life seemed somehow to be brighter.

Mother marvelled at the changes in Grandma. Several years before, she had moved into her daughter's home and settled into a comfortable old age. She was tenderly cared for and lovingly waited on. When the trouble came, Mother had seriously feared for Grandma's life.

But from day one, Grandma determined that she would not be a burden to her family. During the five weeks of the exodus, her endurance increased, and her muscles firmed up. She grew more energetic instead of less. She now handled the cooking, laundry, housecleaning, and child care. Despite the hardships, she remained cheerful and uncomplaining.

Soldiers came to the house after supper that night and called Mother outside. When she came back, the light had gone out of her eyes. The color of their "new" clothes was too bright, she told the girls. They looked like the hated city people. They must not wear them again.

Pitura was beyond tears. Her emotions condensed into a deep ache. Where was Father? Where were her brothers? Where was Chanla's God?

A few days later, another blow fell. The family was ordered to move to another village. Just when they'd made a few friends and life seemed a bit bearable, they must pack their things and move on.

The family was taken to Bosh Tauch village, about three miles from the Vietnamese border. They learned that refugees were frequently moved to prevent them from befriending each other and possibly uniting against their captors. Their house this time was slightly larger, but four families were required to share it. Work continued as before; twelve hours a day, seven days a week.

On his thirteenth birthday, Piteak was the first to become seriously ill. A sudden attack of malaria racked his thin body. The high fever, the chills, and the abdominal cramping totally incapacitated him. The village had no medicine available. Mother and Grandma bathed his fevered brow and comforted him as best they could. Gradually his strength returned.

Soon after Piteak recovered, the grazing area around the village became depleted. Piteak, Pitura, and other older children were ordered to accompany the livestock to an encampment several kilometers away. They would be allowed to come home once a week.

Absolutely frantic, Mother would not allow her eldest daughter, eleven years old, to stay in an army camp with such barbaric men. In desperation, she went to the village leader.

"My oldest daughter is retarded," she told him. "She cannot be trusted away from home for that long. She does not have enough sense to take care of herself."

"She must go," the man said coldly. "We don't have enough to send as it is."

Mother would not give up. "My other son, Prok, could go. He is nearly ten years old and is very bright and responsible."

"We shall see for ourselves if you are telling the truth."

He gestured for two other Khmer Rouge to come with him, and they walked to Mother's house.

As they entered the home, Mother spoke in a loud voice. "My daughter does quite well when supervised, but we cannot trust her out of our sight. She could easily wander away and get lost. Her mind has never been quite right."

Pitura, who had been listening behind the partition, was called. She came slowly, eyes fastened on the ground. The soldiers questioned her, but she continued staring at the floor, saying nothing. She was afraid to speak, afraid to betray her sanity. She picked up a stick and made random marks in the dirt, ignoring them altogether. After watching her for a few minutes, the soldiers seemed satisfied that she was, indeed, simple-minded.

They announced their verdict. Pitura could stay home, but must work in the rice fields with Mother, under her supervision. Younger brother Prok would go with Piteak.

Pitura was almost beside herself with relief. Surely *anything* would be better than caring for those disgusting animals.

Mother's chest tightened as she watched her third and fourth sons leave that afternoon. Faithful, dependable Piteak—how she had come to rely on him! He was the man of the family now, and took the responsibility seriously. And gentle, conscientious Prok did his best to help. Mother worried all week. Would they disappear like the others?

Pitura was skipping a little as she and Mother made their way to the rice field. She felt very grown up, being sent to work with the women.

"Watch the others," Mother instructed. "Do as they do."

Pitura self-consciously removed her sandals, hiked up her skirt, and gingerly stepped into the water. Oh! The water was cold. Ouch, the rocks cut and hurt. The green mud oozed through her toes and engulfed her feet. "At least it smells better than the pig pens," she told Mother.

The sun was up when Pitura felt a strange tickle on her ankle. She lifted her foot and saw a large, bloodsucking leech firmly attached. She screamed for help and ran to dry land. A woman reached over and casually removed the leech, squashing it with her foot. Blood flowed from the wound, and Pitura was hysterical. "You act like a baby," the woman said in disgust.

Pitura looked for her mother, who continued planting rice seedlings as quickly as the other women did. Every now and then someone would stop, pull off a leech, and throw it into the water. Humiliated and frightened, Pitura wondered how she could possibly go back.

A soldier handed her another basket and ordered her to return to work. Pitura seemed rooted to the ground and continued crying.

"Look at the little princess." The guard spit the words out sarcastically. "You like to eat, but you don't like to work. Well, in this place you will not eat unless you work. Get back out there! You are already far behind."

The soldier looked so angry that Pitura grabbed her basket and jumped back into the water, still sobbing. She was slow and clumsy, and her back ached unbearably. She looked pleadingly at Mother, who smiled encouragement. But her eyes said, "Courage, my little one. This is our new life."

"Mother," she said, weeping on the way home that evening, "the rice fields are horrid. I hate those leeches more than I hated the dirty animals."

"Tomorrow will be better," Mother said. "You are much safer here than out in the camps with the men."

"I'd rather be dead than live my life like this! No one cares about us." The family tried to comfort her, but Pitura would not be consoled.

At week's end, Piteak and Prok returned. Although Prok seemed the same as ever, Mother noted a new seriousness tinged with sadness in Piteak. She wondered if he had been punished or mistreated in some way.

That night, after the others were asleep, Piteak told Mother of his terrible experience. He had brought his cattle to a grassy knoll and was sitting under a tree. Prok had fallen asleep on the grass nearby. Hearing voices on the other side of the hill, he crept to the top and peered through the bushes.

He saw two gaunt men, their feet chained together, digging a hole with crude shovels. Two armed soldiers standing nearby shouted obscenities, urged them to hurry, and berated their awkwardness and stupidity. Piteak was afraid to see what would happen, but remained riveted to the scene. His heart went out to those doomed men, not much older than his brothers. When the hole was dug, the prisoners were ordered to sit on the edge while their arms were tied securely behind them. They bent their heads, awaiting the gunfire that would end their misery.

The young soldiers, however, saved their bullets and began clubbing the men with their rifle butts, knocking them into the newly dug grave. Piteak could hear screams and cries as the soldiers rapidly shoveled the dirt back into place, stomping it down firmly. In the horror of the moment, Piteak heaved up his lunch and fainted. Later, he carefully crawled back to his water buffaloes.

While Piteak was away from home, he and Prok stayed in camp with the soldiers. Several befriended them, but one more so than the others. That evening at supper Piteak casually asked if there was another training camp to the north. No one answered his question, but later this soldier friend took him for a walk. Up there, he was told, was a place called Whirling Cloud Death Camp. Men were sent there who were sick or otherwise couldn't carry their full workload, or who resisted the indoctrination of Angka. They were chained in pairs and worked without food until their strength was exhausted. They either eventually died or were killed.

A few weeks later, Piteak's malaria returned. He lay all day in camp, burning with fever, without food or assistance. The soldier who had befriended him walked to his village later that night and brought back Mother. Piteak felt thankful that at least one Khmer Rouge still had a few shreds of compassion!

Mother nursed her son all night and the next day. He improved a bit, and she begged to take him back to the village until he was well. The authorities refused, ordering her to leave Piteak and go back to her own work. Mother pleaded and wept, but was forced to go. She sent up her first tentative appeal to Chanla's God.

Piteak was allowed to return to his village two days later. Mother nursed him at night, and Grandma took over when Mother went to the fields in the morning. Slowly Piteak recovered.

More weeks dragged by. Incessant, backbreaking labor; inadequate food; and recurring illness ravaged them. In the five months since Father, Chanla, and Panno left, they had heard nothing. Surely their menfolk were dead. Mother, Grandma, and the children quit talking in the evenings after work. They were too tired and too sad to think of anything to say. Mother's optimism gradually faded, and she became despondent. She decided there must not be a God after all.

But an ever-caring and watchful heavenly Father had not forgotten them.

Chapter 6
Back to Year Zero

Less than an hour after Father marched off, Chanla and Panno's group was called. Chanla straightened up and stepped firmly forward. Panno followed. And like Father, they did not look back.

Hours passed as they marched; hours of weariness, hunger, worry. A tropical storm burst upon the group, and their pent-up emotions burst forth as well. Tears flowed with the rain as Chanla realized he and his brother were being forced farther and farther from everyone precious to them. Around midnight, the group was led into a large building. Each man was assigned a small space on the floor.

Sometime later, as they tried to sleep, shots rang out. A luckless man on his way to the toilet dropped instantly to the floor, paralyzed with fright.

"No one moves without my permission!" the guard roared. He surveyed the 120 men lying in rows on the bare floor. "Next time I'll shoot to kill."

The stillness was eerie. Panno lay only inches away, but neither brother risked even the softest whisper. Despite the suffocating humidity, Chanla shivered with fear. When his empty stomach rumbled, he looked anxiously at the guard, worrying that the guard might have heard.

Chanla carefully shifted his aching body from time to time. Still wet from the storm, his clothes stuck to him like glue. The night seemed endless. Weariness enveloped his body, but his mind was going full throttle.

Some work detail! Chanla realized he and the others had been marched right into prison.

The next morning, an intensive "reeducation" program began. The meeting started at sunrise and lasted far into the night. The instructors droned on and on as the hours crawled by. Fear kept the men from asking questions. Lack of sleep and the sheer misery of trying to sit still on the ground for so long drained their energies. After some time their brains seemed to shift into automatic and stop filtering the information coming at them.

"The name of our country is now Kampuchea, and our government is Angka," they were told. "We are beginning anew, starting over. *This is the year zero.*

"The Cambodian people have been exploited and enslaved. Your former government leaders were puppets of greedy imperialists who were bleeding the country to benefit foreign empires. But rescue has come. Angka is now in charge!

"Angka is building a new and greater Cambodia, a country without corruption. You are a chosen group, who will be trained to help build this new nation. You must be consumed by this goal. You must think only of Angka, speak only of Angka, work only for Angka, and live only for Angka. Angka is the reason for everything in your lives. Angka will bring *true freedom!* "

Chanla shifted his legs slightly. He wondered if there might be some truth in what was being said. The speaker seemed sincere and earnest. But no one explained what "freedom" was supposed to be.

"Angka has proclaimed the existence of a new disease. It is the sickness of remembering the past, thinking about the previous life. This disease must be wiped out. It will be dealt with harshly wherever it is discovered.

"Angka will tell you what to do and how to do it. You must become like the ox and obey without question. You must have no thought but for the party, no love but for Angka."

During the next few days, Chanla and Panno said little, for they had no privacy. Toilet privileges were granted to only one person at a time. All else was done in groups. They were constantly reminded not to trust anyone, that enemies were everywhere in their midst. The men grew increasingly suspicious of each other.

After seven days of indoctrination, the leaders decided they were ready to work. The camp was divided into groups of ten members each, one of which was appointed captain. Chanla breathed a quick prayer of thanks when he saw that he and Panno were assigned to the same group.

Work began at daybreak. As Chanla got up, he wished he could take a shower. He was still wearing the same clothes from the week before. There was no toothbrush, no comb, no towels, no razors. There was water, however, and he drank gratefully, and washed himself as best he could in the couple of moments he had. Then it was time to go.

Each team worked independently of the others. Chanla's group began by digging irrigation ditches. A nearby team cleared brush. Chanla and Panno later built roads and worked on various construction projects. Whatever Angka ordered, they would do. Each group had an armed guard at all times.

The first meal of the day was served at noon, after which they were allowed a thirty-minute rest. Then they returned to work until dark. Unused to hard physical labor, Chanla feared he would have trouble keeping up, but he soon realized that his team members were displaced city persons as he was. Eventually he learned that one was an accountant, another a lawyer. There were also a taxi driver, a merchant, and a hospital attendant. Most of the men in his group were young.

Chanla was so tired at the end of the first day that he could hardly wait to lie down on his parcel of hard floor. But as the men approached camp they were directed to the indoctrination area. Discussion of their day's work ensued, with criticisms of performance. Reeducation lectures continued far into the night. Finally, near midnight, the men were allowed to eat and sleep.

An exhausted Chanla sank gratefully onto the floor. Never had he worked so hard for so many hours in one day. Sleep came quickly to all of them.

About four days later, Chanla awoke in the night with cramping abdominal pains. With difficulty he aroused the sleeping guard for toilet permission. Other men were having similar problems. It was a difficult night.

By morning, Chanla felt weak and extremely tired, but he dared not complain. He marched to his workplace, wondering how he could get through the day.

The cramps hit again, and Chanla requested toilet privileges. The men were allowed one trip during a six-hour work shift and were required to stay within sight of the guard. Chanla's request was ignored for over an hour. His suffering was acute, and he feared he would faint. When permission came, he walked as far away as he dared. What blessed relief it was just to answer nature's call, to straighten his aching back and have a few moments of rest.

The other men also took advantage of toilet time, badly needing the break. But the guards quickly caught on and changed the rules. The next morning they drew a circle in the dirt a few feet from the work site. That was their toilet for the day. They could go no farther.

Without exception, all the guards smoked cigarettes. They allowed the prisoners who smoked one cigarette break per shift—a total of two per day. Within days, every prisoner, including Chanla, became a smoker. Since they had to make their own cigarettes, the men grew very inventive. Their creations developed into some of the longest and fattest cigarettes known in tobacco history. They savored this small victory.

The food provided at noon for the workers was cooked by old people in nearby villages. They received meager pay, and they cared little about quality. The thin, watery rice gruel they brought usually had few vegetables and an occasional trace of some kind of meat. When mealtime came, these people would dump their kettles of food into a central pot, from which everyone was served. Serving time was limited, so the men ate quickly, and lined up for as many refills as possible. Even so, they were chronically hungry. If there was food left over when serving time ended, the pot and its leftovers remained in the sun and heat all afternoon and evening. That night it would be served again. Rotting spoiled food led to frequent stomach problems and recurring diarrhea.

For the first few days, the teams worked within a twelve-kilometer radius of the camp. Toward the end of the second week, Chanla's group was ordered to move to a more distant site.

Chanla and Panno worked with others to construct a crude shelter. It consisted of four poles driven into the ground; a roof of leaves, straw, and thatch; and no walls. Additional straw was placed on the ground for beds. These shelters provided little protection from the tropical rains. Sometimes the rain would fall all day and all night, sometimes several days and nights. During these times the men worked, ate, and slept soaking wet.

No one had a mosquito net or a sleeping mat. No clothes were issued. Rashes, skin diseases, and open sores abounded. Lice spread quickly to all of them. Their water supply was frequently contaminated. As their bodies weakened, men began dying of malaria, pneumonia, and various other infections. No medical care or medicine was available.

Chanla thought often of his dear, brave father. How was he surviving his ordeal? Chanla no longer resented the tough training he had received. Memories of this wise and disciplined man filled him with new strength and helped him fight his depression.

Although the work, food, and living conditions were scarcely bearable, Chanla dreaded evenings the most. They spent this time in group meetings under the supervision of a guard or Angka official. Besides reviewing and criticizing their day's work, the leader often singled out someone for special attention. Someone might have complained that a worker was not doing his fair share of work. The worker would be denounced as an enemy of Angka and admonished to change his ways. Chanla soon noticed that people who were admonished often mysteriously disappeared.

Officials from Angka headquarters frequently visited the

camps and gave long lectures. Those who had previously lived with little thought or care for the peasants must come forward and confess, they said. Also, people who harbored critical or resentful feelings against Angka must confess. A confession would cleanse the heart and the soul. Angka would forgive. The urging was so intense that several men went forward. Some went out of fear, others hoped to gain favor. But the people who confessed also eventually disappeared.

Chanla and Panno saw and heard things that sickened them. They passed men left in ditches or bomb craters with their elbows tied tightly together behind their backs. In this position it was difficult to breathe, and most did not live long. They heard cries and shots in the night, and frequently passed unburied, decomposing bodies.

Always within earshot of a guard, they were constantly watched. Reporting on one's fellow prisoners was rewarded. Chanla and Panno quickly learned to see nothing, hear nothing, and speak nothing. Never say "no," they learned, and always say "yes." They were careful not to irritate fellow workers, who might denounce them out of spite at the evening meetings. These were the elements of survival.

Only in his mind could Chanla retain his freedom. He repeated Bible promises, sang hymns, and continually prayed for his family. Thus he fought the darkness and despair that threatened to engulf him.

Weeks, then months went by. They were moved from place to place. Unrelenting, backbreaking work stretched from sunrise to sunset, seven days a week, with no variation. Evenings continued to be filled with admonitions, criticisms, threats, and propaganda. They had no freedom and absolutely no privacy.

Since the men never received enough food, they grew thinner and weaker. One night Chanla realized he could no longer see the stars. Checking with Panno and others, he discovered they had the same problem. Chanla remembered studying about night blindness and vitamin deficiency and worried that he might go completely blind.

During the third month, Panno came down with malaria

and stomach cramps. The cramps became so severe that one night Panno cried out several times. Chanla feared for his brother's life. Men had been shot for lesser disturbances. Finding some leaves with herbal qualities, Chanla ground them up and added them to his brother's food. Surprisingly, Panno improved.

Constant suspicion, fear, hunger, and fatigue led the men to withdraw more and more into themselves. They seldom spoke, and no one smiled. Chanla looked at the blank, numb faces about him and realized how truly they had become like oxen. No longer did anyone have the energy to resist. They were little more than machines, moving to the will of their captors.

Chanla, however, continued to pray to God. Throughout the day, in his mind, he poured out his worries, hopes, and disappointments to his heavenly Father. He thought about his family and prayed for them. His captors had control of his physical body, but he would not give them his mind.

One morning the brothers were leaning over a water pot a few feet from the others. "Several are planning to escape," Panno whispered. "I want to go. I'm not going to live much longer if I stay in this camp."

"No, Panno, no!" Chanla was surprised at his own forcefulness. "Not yet. Don't try it yet." The last words were a plea. Chanla knew his brother had not recovered from his illness. Panno was deeply depressed, forcing his weak body through the pain and punishment of his daily work.

Chanla was strongly tempted to feel that an escape attempt with a probable quick death might be preferable to dying as slowly and painfully as they were now doing. But he remembered Father's words, "You must take care of the others."

"God," he breathed, "thank You for reminding me that the family needs me." He knew he must survive for them.

Several days later, two men from Chanla's team were marched outside the camp and executed. Seven more were taken from other teams. Panno dismissed further thoughts of escape.

At the end of four months, a uniformed official appeared

and announced that the men were now rehabilitated. They would be released in two days. Hope returned to the prisoners' hearts, though they carefully concealed any show of emotion.

Two weeks passed, and they were transferred to another camp. There they were forced to work into the night hours and were given even less food. Malnutrition and disease continued its terrible toll. Hope of release dimmed, then disappeared.

Chanla worried about his ailing brother. He realized that they would be worked until they eventually died. Life became a grim battle for the barest survival. The brothers ate leaves, weeds, even insects. Their bodies screamed for rest as they were mercilessly pressed to increase work quotas. Chanla tried to pray and to think of his family, but hunger and weariness consumed him. Food and rest became an obsession. He remembered his father's stories about his survival during the Japanese occupation. He no longer dismissed them as exaggerations. He knew they were real.

One day Chanla, Panno, and several others were returned to the large holding center where they'd been separated from Father. Other prisoners from various camps were there too, but the two brothers did not find Father. After three days of intense indoctrination, Chanla and Panno were pronounced rehabilitated and told they could return to their families.

"Let's go, boys," a big voice boomed behind them. They were surprised to find the village sheriff waiting to escort them "home." It was the same man who had brought them to this place five months before. He mounted his bicycle and led the way. As before, they trotted along behind.

Bits of hope edged into Chanla's heart as the miles went by. Was his family safe? That was his prayer. It would be enough.

He could not have imagined the treasure Mother would have for him when he returned.

Chapter 7
Chanla's Treasure

As Mother walked toward the rice field in the early dawn, she saw the sheriff approaching on his bicycle. She looked away, hoping he would not recognize her. Pitura had not been ready, and Mother worried that her tardiness would be noticed and punished.

The sheriff, however, pulled up right beside her.

"Good news, woman!" he announced loudly. Then, starting off again, he yelled over his shoulder, "I'm bringing your sons back tonight."

What? Had she heard correctly? Her sons—coming home? She wondered if it could be true. Or was it just another cruel hoax? Months of heavy labor and continual disappointments had taught her not to trust Angka's promises. Yet a streak of hope pierced through her dark despair.

When Pitura caught up with her a few moments later, she shared the news with her. Pitura stared, unwilling to believe.

"Is it true? Do you think it will really happen?" Pitura sounded so forlorn that Mother could not hold back an amused smile, and her eyes began to sparkle.

"I don't know for sure, dear one. But it was the same sheriff who took them away." She smiled again. "I have a feeling that it's going to happen. One thing worries me, though." Mother looked serious again. "The sheriff said he was bringing home my *sons*. What about Father? Surely

63

he will bring Father as well."

Pitura recovered quickly. "Of course he meant Father. He took them away together, didn't he?"

Their steps lightened, and their hands flew up and down the rows of rice plants that morning. Mother's mind was brimming with plans. She would unpack their sleeping mats and place fresh clothes beside them. She saw two children playing nearby and sent them scurrying to carry the news to Grandma and the others. For Mother and Pitura, the day couldn't pass fast enough.

When Mother and Pitura got home, the place was spotless. Grandma was cooking extra bits of food the children had scrounged up that afternoon.

Near sundown, the family spotted the sheriff and his two charges approaching. Chanla and Panno both rushed toward Mother and knelt on the ground at her feet. They gave her the highest honor a Cambodian could pay to another person, and both boys felt such a depth of love and respect for their mother that it was perfectly appropriate.

As Chanla rose and hugged his mother, he saw the mixture of joy, shock, and horror in her eyes as she hugged him. He suddenly realized how pitiful he and Panno must look—bony skeletons in the filthy, tattered remnants of the clothes they'd worn continuously for five months. Unshaven, they had long, matted hair, and itching patches of skin disease blackened parts of their arms and legs. But none of that mattered now. Tears flowed freely as Mother, Grandmother, brothers, and sisters hugged and kissed and held each other.

Only one question clouded the reunion. Finally Mother voiced it. "Where is Father?" Chanla and Panno told of their separation and suggested he might yet be coming. They must be patient.

Chanla and Panno went to bathe. Soap! It was a small piece, but it was real soap! They realized now how much they'd missed it. And clean clothes! No king in his royal robes ever felt finer than Chanla and Panno did as they put on fresh clean clothes that night. They shaved and gave each other quick haircuts. Mother soothed their itching skin lesions with a mixture of seeds, coconut oil, and ground herbs. For the first time in months, they experienced relief.

For Chanla, the simple meal that Grandma prepared that night was the finest feast he could remember. Pitura sat as close as possible to Chanla, and bubbly little Reni staked out the other side. Chande curled up in his lap. Vivatny and Prok claimed Panno, and Piteak sat shyly nearby. Pitura told her brothers about the leeches and showed them the scars on her legs.

During the meal, Chanla mentioned that they had seen their great-uncle march off with Father's group. When they finished eating, the whole family rushed over to his house to see if he, too, had been released. But he had not.

As they walked home, Mother slipped her arms around her sons. They sensed her struggle. Glad for them, she nevertheless felt a growing, gnawing fear inside her. "Look, Mother," Chanla said, "you know Father. He's a wise man, and he's tough. He knows how to survive."

"He'll be released in the next group," Panno added. "These things take time."

"In the meantime, let's celebrate our present blessings." Chanla picked up his smallest sister, tossed her in the air, and caught her in a big hug. Mother began to relax, and small smiles again tugged at her lips.

Mother told about their experiences at the pagoda, and the loss of the motorcycle. She had turned in their radio, lest it be found and the family punished.

It was late, and the children had fallen asleep. Chanla unrolled his sleeping mat and arranged his mosquito net. He turned to watch Mother reach for her pillow and remove an object from inside. She placed it in Chanla's hands.

It was wrapped in muslin, but he knew immediately what it was. His Bible! Surprise gave way to amazement as Chanla realized the risk she had taken for him. If discovered, Mother could have been tortured and shot. Neither spoke, but the unclouded joy in her son's eyes was ample reward.

Mother had strung up a few curtains, giving the family

a degree of privacy in the crowded house. With light from a small oil lamp, Chanla squatted behind the partition and opened his Bible. It was actually only half a Bible. During the hectic days of the exodus, he and a Christian cousin discovered they had one small Bible between them. Chanla had torn it in half. Chanla's part contained the New Testament and part of the Old, to Isaiah. He had wrapped it in a piece of cloth and hidden it in his clothes, fearing to tell Mother.

Chanla realized that Mother had understood, and the little book had been preserved. Love and respect for this quiet, courageous woman sprang up from his heart. He opened the Bible to the apostle Paul's letter to the Philippians. Paul had been a prisoner when he wrote these words. *He* knew what it was like to suffer. Chanla felt comforted as he read Paul's words of thanksgiving and faith: "*I know that this will turn out for my salvation . . .*"

"Yes, dear God," Chanla prayed, "make this experience work out for my salvation and for the salvation of my family. This is my heart's desire. And comfort and bless Father." Chanla lay on his mat under a mosquito net with his head on a pillow. Ahhh—it felt like heaven!

The next morning, the sheriff was at the door. Chanla looked up with dismay. Were they to be taken away again?

The sheriff explained that work needed to be done on the farms surrounding the village. The two boys were needed. However, they would be allowed to return to their families in the evening.

This last concession softened the blow. Somehow the sun seemed brighter and the sky bluer that day as Chanla and Panno left with the other men of the village.

Work on the farms was not as difficult as in the prison camp, and time passed quickly. They spent their evenings playing with the children and visiting quietly with the family. Grandma outdid herself, producing meals with many variations, considering the meager rations she had to work with. Mother began smiling again and even laughing out loud.

Pitura clung to her brothers, their presence and comfort

somehow helping to fill her empty life of loneliness and isolation. They tickled her and teased her, commenting on her budding good looks. Pitura laughed and brushed her hair and put on her prettiest dresses after work. No one discouraged her, and fortunately, no one reported her.

Each evening after supper, the children gathered around Chanla for stories. He told them the story of Daniel, the young prince who had been taken captive by a mighty king. But God took care of him, even in the lions' den. He told them about Ruth and about Queen Esther and the story of Naaman and the captive maid. Chanla noticed that Mother and Grandma sat nearby, listening.

Chanla slept better than he had in months. With his own mat and pillow, clean clothes, and his little Bible to read, life seemed almost normal. He even wondered, in some vague way, if perhaps Angka did have some good intentions for the country. The village was peaceful, and an abundant harvest was coming. With his family nearly restored, he felt he could bear almost anything. Although their life was still far from ideal, Chanla realized that his family was fortunate in comparison to most of the others. He now spoke openly about God and about his faith.

On the fifth night, around 2:00 a.m., Panno's illness struck again. He shook with chills, then burned with fever. His stomach cramped so badly he moaned aloud. But this time he was not left alone to suffer on the cold ground. Mother sponged his burning body, and Pitura applied cool cloths to his head. Chanla mixed herbs and leaves into tea, which helped the cramps. When the others were at work during the day, Grandma and the small sisters took care of him.

That same night, Piteak sat up suddenly, drenched with sweat. His heart raced at breakneck speed as he looked around at his family, especially his two older brothers. The nightmare had returned. Once again he was hearing the heart-wrenching screams of the two young men being clubbed into graves and buried alive by the guards.

He stared into the darkness. Would he be haunted forever by what he had seen? He decided not to mention his nightmare to anyone. The family had to cope with enough sorrow and pain as it was.

Father's absence continued to worry them. The family questioned every visitor, newcomer, and returned prisoner who came to the village. No one had seen him or heard any news.

About a month after the boys had come home, Mother was sent on an errand to a nearby village. On her way back, she observed several men at work in a large field. She carefully scanned the group. Mother did this whenever she saw men working, always hoping somehow, sometime to recognize a loved one. But so far, she had not found anyone she knew.

This time, however, she spotted a familiar figure. Could it be? No, it couldn't, but—yes, it was—*Father!* He was not facing in her direction, but she could see his outline from the back and side very clearly. He was about 100 meters away. His movements, his profile, his posture, the way he swung his hoe were unmistakable. *It was Father!*

She felt like shouting for joy. She longed to call to him, to throw something to try getting his attention, but she knew better. Such actions could get them both killed. In fact, she dared not act unusually at all. A guard stood only a few feet from Father. There was no way she could approach him without attracting unwanted attention.

Mother walked as slowly as she dared, hoping Father would look up. She adjusted her load and used every delaying tactic she could think of. But Father worked with single-minded attention to his job.

Mother rushed home to share the good news with the others. Chanla was at work camp, and Panno was still recuperating. That night she sent a young nephew to the nearest camp headquarters with a package of food and tobacco. As one of the original villagers, he was allowed more freedom than the displaced city people.

Officers at the camp accepted the package, but refused to let the boy see Father. In fact, they would not admit that he was there. Mother, however, kept sending small packages of food, clothing, and tobacco. She asked Chanla to pray that Father would receive them.

On his fourth trip, the nephew returned with the package. The officers told him that Father had been transferred to another camp, but refused to tell him its name or location.

A few days later, Great-Uncle returned home. When the word reached the Dok family, they went over to his home for news.

"Your father was not included in the group to be released because he was ill," he reported. "He had a serious case of dysentery."

"He'll get well, Mother," Chanla said. "He's a strong man. We'll keep praying for him."

"He'll probably be along in a few days." Panno tried to sound reassuring.

Although the brothers spoke confidently, they felt a chilling fear. They knew that guards were not patient with sick men.

Mother decided to find Father herself. Great-Uncle described the location of the camp, and Mother obtained permission to take food and supplies to her sick husband.

After miles of travel, Mother located the camp, but was told the Dok Savang was not there. She insisted that he had been there a few days before, as Great-Uncle had seen him. Annoyed, they finally told her he had been taken to the provincial hospital. She went to the hospital, but they had not heard of him. She visited every camp and hospital she could find in the region, but no one had seen him.

Several nights later, Great-Uncle approached Chanla. "Perhaps I should have mentioned it earlier," he said, "but before I left camp I overheard some guards talking about your father. They mentioned a place. I have no idea where it is, only its name: 'Whirling Cloud.'"

Chanla felt a surge of excitement. "Whirling Cloud Camp? Are you sure?"

"I think so. It was such an unusual name that it stuck in my mind."

Chanla was elated and immediately told Panno. With the name of the camp, they should be able to locate Father. They would surprise their tired, worried mother!

Chapter 8
The Productivity Army

"Oh, oh, here come the soldiers," said Pitura, who was looking out the window. It was the seventh night since Chanla and Panno had come home.

The black-pajama-clad Khmer Rouge stepped up to the door. "We are here to conscript you into the new Productivity Army," they announced with bland cheerfulness, as though delivering welcome news. They looked around at the young men in the house. "Every able-bodied man, fifteen years and up, is included."

Mother showed them Panno, who was still very ill— cramping and vomiting blood. He was temporarily exempted. Mother was given permission to stay home and care for him.

Chanla, however, had to go. This time he was able to pack a few necessities. The next morning, the children clung to him, crying. Pitura took it especially hard.

"I just can't live much longer like this," she told him, sobbing on his shoulder. "I'd rather die."

Chanla hugged her, patting her head and rubbing her shoulders. "Dear sister, I'm sorry you have to work so hard, but don't give up. Things can't get much worse. They're going to get better."

"I want to believe you. You seem so courageous." Pitura wiped her eyes. "Is it your God who makes you this way?"

"My God comforts and encourages me. Yes, I'm sure that He gives me special strength." His arm tightened

71

around her. "It won't last forever. Be patient. Keep hope in your heart. I will pray for you."

The harvest that year was abundant, and the Productivity Army fanned out over the countryside to gather it in. Their work was close to the village, and Chanla could frequently slip home for the night.

As the warehouses filled with rice, rations were liberalized. People who had lived for months on food fit only for pigs began to enjoy "good rice" once more. What rejoicing! Panno improved, and everyone felt better.

"Warehouses are overflowing with rice. There will be plenty for us all," said Mother, smiling at her family. Their hard work had paid off.

"I'm so tired of being hungry," said Pitura.

"My stomach has felt empty every day this whole year," sighed Piteak.

Unfortunately, the bonanza was brief. Although improved in quality, their rations were again cut. The Khmer Rouge explained that in other regions the harvest had not been good, and they must share their bounty. The people had to choke back their frustration and helplessness as they watched large convoys of trucks haul away the precious products of their labor.

Chanla's group moved from place to place as their work required. Sometimes they slept in tents or buildings, but often they slept out in the open, exposed to the elements. As before, they had only bits of straw for beds, no mosquito nets, and often no protection from the elements. Workdays were the same, from predawn to dusk, seven days a week. Evenings were filled with productivity reports, critiques of their work, and the never-ending indoctrination sessions they'd endured in prison. Chanla felt compensated, however, by the fact that he could frequently see his family. He would leave camp late at night and return before the rising bell clanged at 4:00 a.m.

In evening sessions, Chanla learned about the massive reorganization occurring in his country. Everything was directed by a faceless, all-powerful *Angka*. Angka was actually a high central committee in Phnom Penh responsible for all decisions and all laws. Months later, General Pol Pot and his ally, General Ieng Sary, emerged as the leaders behind the movement. Pol Pot was half-Chinese and half-Cambodian. Ieng Sary was a Cambodian who had received his education in North Vietnam.

Originally Cambodian peasants and farmers, the Khmer Rouge were equipped and indoctrinated by the North Vietnamese, then by the Chinese. During the 1975 Cambodian revolution, the long enmity between the countries came to a head, and the Vietnamese were driven out of Cambodia. In the midst of reorganizing their own postwar country, the Vietnamese offered little resistance.

The present Khmer Rouge dressed like Chinese peasants, with Chinese-style caps, black clothes, and rubber-tire sandals. They always wore the distinctive red scarf somewhere on their body. Angka divided Cambodia, now called Kampuchea, into eight regions, each with twenty provinces. Each province contained seven to eight districts, and a district was divided into five or six sections. The sections, in turn, were composed of villages and hamlets. Every citizen was assigned by Angka to a specific hamlet or village. Trespassing outside an assigned area without permits was punished, often severely.

As harvest time ended, Chanla and the others in the Productivity Army began building communes. Villagers as well as workers were forced to move into these large buildings, which had no partitions or privacy. Some families were allowed to live in the few houses that still stood, but were crowded in so tightly that conditions were little better.

Large central kitchens were built, and soon private cooking, a treasured privilege, was abolished.

"You are so fortunate," their captors said. "You don't have to cook. Your meals are here waiting for you. Now you will have many more hours to work for Angka." To enforce this, the Khmer Rouge searched each family's belongings, collecting every eating utensil, cooking pot, and small stove they could find. They also confiscated clothing and most other possessions, leaving only the barest necessities. Pajamalike outfits of crude black material were issued, and everyone soon looked alike.

Grandmother was sent to weave baskets with other old people. The tiny tots played about the village.

In these ways they abolished almost all semblance of family life. Work was everything. The soldiers put the people's property in a central warehouse to be kept by Angka. Livestock was seized at will, and local farmers who had owned their homes and land for generations were required to "give it to the people." Their families were forced to move into the communes. If anyone complained, his crops were burned, or he was imprisoned or executed.

Long ago Mother had sewn their jewelry, gold, and other valuables into secret pockets and cloth belts, which they wore at all times around their bodies under their clothes. Even Chanla and Panno carried a few valuables with them in case of emergency.

When Chanla came home, he found Mother less upset over the changes than he expected. His family was still living in their "house."

"Chanla," she confided with a twinkle, "I was able to hide most of our utensils, a bundle of Father's possessions, and your Bible. They let us keep our sleeping mats, pillows, and mosquito nets."

One day Pitura saw a Khmer Rouge woman wearing one of her blouses, and the dam broke. Pitura wept uncontrollably on Mother's shoulder. She felt personally violated. A few days later, however, Chanla slipped into the family's living space, chuckling.

"Why are you laughing?" Pitura demanded.

Chanla looked at her, trying to constrain his mirth. "I passed a very fat soldier out there wearing one of my shirts," Chanla said. "All but one of the buttons had popped off." Chanla doubled up again.

Pitura smiled slightly, then giggled, and finally began laughing too. From then on, the family made a point of joking privately when they saw their captors display any of their belongings. It cleared the air.

Despite their cruelty and arrogance, the Khmer Rouge followed certain codes. They scorned corruption and material possessions, and they could not be bribed. The working people, the peasants, received a degree of respect.

Unless they were denounced and imprisoned, the women were safe from rape and molestation, and neither men nor women were bodily searched.

Their possessions, however, were a different matter. These belonged to Angka, along with their labor, their loyalties, and their thoughts. This kind of total dedication, they were told, would make Kampuchea the greatest nation in the world.

Early the next year, another reorganization took place. The population was divided into three groups: *Group I* people consisted of younger, unmarried men and women, approximately fifteen to thirty-five years old; *Group II* were the married people and families; *Group III* were the old people, the sick and crippled, and the children.

As Mother nursed Panno, he grew stronger and eventually was able to join the *Group III* people, who wove baskets, made rope, did the cooking, repaired machinery, cared for livestock, and generally tended to village needs.

Mother continued to worry about Father. Chanla and Panno tried to encourage her. "Father is a rugged and resolute man," they reminded her. "He will recover and return, just as we did." Although the boys talked optimistically, deep down their own hopes were fading. They had asked everywhere, but no one they spoke to had heard of Whirling Cloud Camp.

In February 1976, all the Group I people were conscripted into labor camps, both men and women, though they were housed separately. They would build roads, construct dams, dig canals, and plant the spring rice. Rules tightened. They received few opportunities to leave camp and visit families. During the rainy season, the men were often forced to rise at 2:00 or 3:00 a.m. and continue working into the night. Rations were cut back until Chanla was reminded of prison days. The men and women were so weakened by hunger and fatigue, they could think of little else. Discipline was severe, and sick men were forced to work until they dropped. Many died.

Mother and Pitura continued their twelve-hour workdays under a relentless sun. Thirteen-year-old Piteak, nine-year-old Prok, and seven-year-old Reni trekked to the village each morning. They received one hour of what passed for "schooling," actually indoctrination, and spent the rest of the day tending the village livestock.

Reni loved her job. She had a special way with animals, giving each one a name. She talked to them and sang them little songs. At night she unfailingly returned each animal to its proper owner. Her smiles and sunny disposition endeared her to the villagers as well as to her family. On her eighth birthday nearly everyone in town spoke to her and wished her well. She was a charmer already. One night in late March, Mother heard her daughter calling.

"M-mom-my, I'm free—zing." Mother found Reni shaking with a chill. She wrapped her and held her until the fever came. Then she sponged her and fanned her gently. In the morning she called Piteak.

"Go to the village leader and tell him Reni is very ill. Ask him to please excuse me from work to care for her."

When Piteak returned, the sheriff was right behind him. "Are you out of your mind, woman?" he bellowed. "This is rice-planting season, and we do not have enough hands as it is. You must work. The old lady can take care of the kid."

Grandma sponged the fevered body. No medicines were available, but kindly village people helped harvest tender leaves from the guava trees. Grandma made tea out of these leaves and pieces of bark. The family used these and other Cambodian folk remedies for the fever and diarrhea.

Four days went by and Reni was no better. Mother spent most of the night nursing her and again begged to stay home. Again she was ordered back to the fields. Exhausted and panic-stricken, she sent an urgent message to Chanla to come home. He did not come. Mother herself went to his superiors and begged them to allow Chanla to see his sister before she died.

On the seventh day, a messenger came for Mother in the rice field. She rushed home to find several old women around her house, wailing loudly. Reni had died in convulsions an hour earlier. Her last words had been calls for Mother. Chanla was not there. Mother found out later that he had not even heard of his sister's illness.

The family was devastated. Quick funerals were necessary in this hot, humid country. Cambodians historically cremate their dead, but the family was too disheartened to attempt this ceremony, especially with Panno ill and Chanla gone. Two cousins helped sorrowing Piteak dig a little grave near a stand of trees. Mother tenderly bathed and perfumed Reni's small body, brushed her hair, and wrapped her in the finest piece of material she had left. If only Father were there. If only she had stayed home that day. If only. . . . She hugged the little girl for the last time. She longed for Chanla's strength and comfort, and wished he could be there to ask his God to receive Reni's spirit. The family lighted some pieces of incense that Mother located, since they had no candles.

The loss of Reni was more than Mother could bear. How could she face life without Reni's little smiles and happy songs? Reni was her most affectionate child. She had generously lavished hugs and kisses on the whole family. Sometimes she had crept to Mother in the night and cuddled close, pressing her cheek against Mother's. What a comfort this little sunbeam had been to her struggling mother!

With her husband gone and her oldest son beyond reach, Mother reached her limit. She withdrew to her sleeping mat and refused to be consoled. Even the Khmer Rouge left her alone for the rest of the week.

Added to this burden, the attitude of the villagers suddenly changed. Reni had had an evil spirit, they decided. No normal person conversed with animals. They concluded that the spirits had killed her. The people had no strong religious roots, and superstition was rampant. The fearful villagers no longer spoke to the family. Sorrow and gloom enveloped them like a dense fog.

About two weeks later, the "new people" were once again notified that they must move to another village, Het Sam Nanh, a hamlet several kilometers away. Although adjusting to unfamiliar places was always hard, Mother welcomed this change. Once more they packed their things, thankful for the one bicycle they still had.

At Het Sam Nanh they were assigned a house that three other families already occupied. The people grudgingly made room for them, grumbling all the while.

Two months after Reni's death, Panno recovered sufficiently to join his brother's Productivity unit. By this time, the Khmer Rouge were delegating considerable responsibility to the "old people," the peasants who had lived their lives in the villages. These people had coexisted for several years with the Khmer Rouge, and, if only for their own protection, had sympathized with them and helped them as they could. As a reward, the "old people" were gradually promoted to positions of greater responsibility. It became evident that no "new people" could hope for promotions or betterment of their situation beyond the most menial of jobs.

In Chanla's camp, as in others, "old people" began to serve as guards and overseers. The same held true in the villages. The Khmer Rouge assumed positions at the sectional levels and above. In addition, "squads," or "patrols," of Khmer Rouge roamed about keeping check on things, executing discipline, and picking up prisoners. They also lectured at important indoctrination sessions if higher officials were not present.

The supervision by the "old people" was a bit more lax. A worker, for instance, could slip away after the evening "class" and visit his family, provided he was present and ready to work when the rising bell rang next morning. No one could be missing from his group, and quotas must be reached, or punishment was severe.

As pressures in some areas eased, cruelty and oppression worsened in others. If any mistake was made, if any tool was missing, if a quota wasn't met, a scapegoat must be found and punished—even tortured and executed. This could happen if a person simply irritated one of his superiors. In Chanla's group, a young man, a Christian, somehow acquired a guitar. Before going to bed at night, he would sit and strum the song "This Little Light of Mine" a couple of times. He continued playing the piece night after night. Someone reported him.

A few days later, he was sent on an errand to a nearby

village. He was never seen again. The rumor circulated that he had been ambushed and executed along the way by a Khmer Rouge "squad."

Panno continued working in the labor camps for the next four months. But the hard work and starvation rations again drained his strength. His illness returned with a vengeance.

Panno was a likable young man. Even his captors responded to his friendliness, good humor, and youthful enthusiasm. He was not treated as harshly as some of the other sick men, who were either left to suffer alone in the barracks or were transferred to death camps. Chanla requested permission to take him home and received it.

Mother nursed Panno with all her love, skill, and devotion, but this time he did not improve. Every bone in his body ached incessantly, and he was racked by chills and fevers. Abdominal cramps were unrelenting, and bloody discharges continued. It became difficult for him to breathe.

Fearing for his life. Mother begged for permission to take him to the village hospital. Because he was so ill, he was transferred to a sectional hospital, and then to a provincial hospital. None of these hospitals had trained medical personnel or even the simplest medications. He was treated with powders ground from rice, grain, bark, roots, and leaves of certain herbs. Food supplies were no better than at the villages, where rations had returned to starvation levels within a few weeks after the harvest.

After two months in the hospital, Panno requested permission to go home. He wanted to spend his last days with his family. During this time, a great many people were dying from starvation, dysentery, tuberculosis, malaria, exhaustion, brutality, and the continuing executions being carried out by the Khmer Rouge.

As Panno grew increasingly delirious and listless, Mother became frantic. Father was right. He had said the Khmer Rouge would work them until they all died. Her family was going, one by one, and she could do nothing about it.

Mother struggled with conflicting emotions; a desire to

believe in Chanla's God, contrasted with her lifelong Buddhist background. Finally, in desperation, she clasped her hands together and raised her eyes upward. "Chanla's God," she pleaded, "there is no one left who can help Panno. Will *You* help him?"

"*Can* You help him?"

Chapter 9
Relief From the East

Armed with renewed hope, Mother implored the officials one last time to allow Chanla to come home before his brother died. Miraculously, this time they agreed. Chanla's compassionate heart went out to Panno as he saw the pale, emaciated skeleton he had become. Panno aroused enough to recognize Chanla, but was only dimly aware of his surroundings.

Determined that Panno must have more nourishing food, Chanla and his brothers and sisters scoured the surrounding countryside for edible plants, berries, and roots. This was extremely dangerous, but Panno's needs overwhelmed their fears.

Mother begged for extra rice from the communal kitchen. She had made many friends in the new village, and Panno was also known and well-liked. Panno's illness had committed him, much of the time, to working with the old people and children in the village. His cheerfulness, good humor, and friendliness paid off now. The guard in the kitchen allowed extra rations. Village people secretly brought small offerings. Mother and Pitura caught crabs in the rice fields and slipped them into their pockets. The little girls trapped small minnows in old cans. Panno began to respond. Gradually he gained strength and recovered.

Conditions in the village and surrounding countryside, however, were deteriorating. Restless and tense, the

81

Khmer Rouge began to fight among themselves. Purges grew more severe, and the village people received heavier workloads and higher quotas.

Dismayed, Chanla noted that the irrigation canals they'd dug the previous year had not withstood the rainy season. Most of them had washed out, endangering much of the rice crop. They did not have the tools or machines to do a proper job. Such things were capitalistic junk, they were told. But Chanla could not see how the people were supposed to build a modern nation with only buckets, shovels, and hoes.

The arrival of a Jeep in the village one day signaled an opportunity for those who wished to relocate in a more prosperous section of the country. Soldiers promised them plenty of rice and individual houses. As the people considered their harsh living conditions and starvation rations, they wanted to believe the story. What did they have to lose? All their possessions could be carried in a few small bundles.

The promises sounded so good and the urging was so great that about 100 families signed up to go. Chanla was at labor camp, but the rest of the family urged Mother to sign up also.

"No," Mother said firmly. "We are not going anywhere without Father."

When Chanla heard of it, he agreed with Mother, not so much because of hope for Father, but because he instinctively distrusted the Khmer Rouge. Later, they heard that after traveling about fifty kilometers down the road, the people had been ordered out of the trucks and executed—men, women, and children. This was Angka's message to those who complained or were dissatisfied with their circumstances.

One night the family heard agonizing cries coming from near the river. These continued for some time before slowly dying away. No one dared investigate or ask questions. The next day Panno, recovered sufficiently to rejoin the local work force, was sent on an errand to the next village. Beside the river he passed a pile of charred remains. It appeared to be a family. Apparently they had been bound, ignited, and burned alive. Panno shuddered, wondering what they had done to offend their captors.

Helicopter blades beat the early morning air like a throbbing heart. The sound was coming closer. Chanla and Piteak crept to the window and looked out. The rest of the family remained rooted to their sleeping mats.

Chanla saw a large Huey helicopter skimming in over the treetops. An American flag was painted on its side, and he could make out the outline of the pilot talking into his headset.

"They are coming to rescue us," Chanla shouted to the others. "We must go meet them."

He stepped out into the backyard and watched the giant helicopter descend. It would take them to America! It would take them to freedom!

"Let's go," he yelled to his family. He grasped Grandma's arm and picked up little Chande. They all ran toward the helicopter. The door opened, and the pilot motioned for them to hurry.

A mosquito whined loudly in Chanla's right ear, and he slapped at it. He opened his eyes in the darkness. His family slept peacefully about him. The shock of reality came on him slowly. There was no helicopter, no rescue, no hope of freedom.

What a strange dream! Never before had Chanla or any family member even dreamed of leaving their own country. They had always envisioned this nightmare passing and Cambodia becoming normal once more. Until then, they were determined to adapt and try to survive. How could they ever hope to be happy as foreigners in a strange land?

Freedom. Chanla pondered the word wearily. During the past few years he had heard many people use the word, in the same breath promising freedom, a better life, greater prosperity, true equality—over and over again. Yet they kept experiencing less freedom, more oppression, increasing poverty, and continuing starvation. Equality didn't exist. The Khmer Rouge were absolute rulers, taking what they wanted and making slaves of the others. Each day brought more pain, illness, torture, and death. The future of Cambodia looked very bleak indeed.

Chanla had heard of refugees escaping into Red Cross camps along the border with Thailand. It was a treacherous route with great risks. Many lost their lives. But those who succeeded received their *freedom*, a new chance at life. Chanla tried to imagine what freedom would be like. To go home at night without first securing permission. To be able to grow one's own rice and eat it. To wear a colored shirt, and face a new day without the dread of torture and execution. Freedom sounded good. The word took root in his mind.

Chanla casually mentioned his dream to Mother the next morning. He made light of it, not wanting to worry her, but his intention was to elicit her reaction.

"Well, Chanla," she said, "even if we could escape, we wouldn't go without Father."

During the last half of 1977, the new regime began to unravel. Despite the Khmer Rouge's high-sounding dreams and big plans, the country was going downhill. Infighting developed among the leaders. One by one, many of them were denounced, tortured, and executed. Those at higher levels blamed their failures on those under them. The ones at the sectional, district, and village levels vented their anger on the people.

Their code kept the Khmer Rouge from abusing the peasants openly. But if any person could be accused of breaking a rule, making a "mistake," hiding anything, telling a lie, harboring resentful thoughts, plotting escape or even thinking about it, he was hauled off to "prison," where his guilt was determined and punishment meted out. An angry or jealous person might denounce or inform on another, and that person could be marched away with no checking, no proof, not even an explanation. Uttering even the smallest complaint was often construed as a betrayal of the Communist regime.

Once a person was denounced or suspected of being an enemy, an "escort" would arrive to take him or her to prison. Suspects were tied, usually with elbows together behind their backs, and marched off at bayonet point.

Though "purges" usually occurred in the evenings as workers came in from the fields, sometimes people would vanish in the night or while on an errand.

Often several people were targeted at one time. Soldiers bound them hand and foot, leaving them to wait at the village outskirts until they could gather the rest of the victims. Though villagers sometimes spotted friends or relatives in the condemned group, they dared not speak to them or even show any recognition, lest they too be taken.

Often these prisoners did not even reach the prison camps. Once out of sight of the village, they would be beaten, killed with axes or hoes, or sometimes shot. They were rarely buried. Their bodies would be left to rot, or kicked into the river. Floating corpses became a common sight. Dogs sometimes dragged mutilated body parts into the village, fighting over the remains.

Chanla saw a corpse hanging upside down from a tree with its eyes burned out. Several times he and Panno saw human heads hanging from trees or mounted on stakes. No one dared say anything or even appear to notice. The Khmer Rouge used these tactics to keep the people in line and to assure that the people accorded them unquestioned obedience and proper respect.

Rumors circulated about events in prisons. People feared being killed much more than they feared dying from disease or starvation. Those unfortunate enough to reach the prison camps found the procedures unvarying.

Prisoners heard the accusations against them read aloud. Charges against women ranged from stealing food from the common kitchen or hiding personal treasures to being the wife or favored consort of a politician, soldier, or government worker in the former regime. The men were accused of fomenting trouble, insubordination, plotting to escape, laziness, or being spies. If all else failed, charges could be contrived, such as hiding their true identities or former occupations. Officials promised them that if they would confess and tell the truth, Angka would forgive and they would be cleansed. They even occasionally hinted that those who confessed would be elevated in status. If the person did confess, however, everything changed.

"Aha! So you admit it. You are guilty. You must be punished to the full extent of the law."

Those who denied the charges, who tried to prove their innocence, were likewise blasted.

"You are lying. We know you are lying. We have proof!" But none was produced. These people would also be sentenced to the maximum penalty.

The people quickly learned to deny everything. Those who confessed and sought the promised forgiveness and cleansing were never seen again. The Khmer Rouge considered them weak, worthless individuals who could not be trusted to keep their mouths shut or be loyal to the new regime. A person who maintained his innocence would occasionally survive the ordeal and return to his village.

Condemned prisoners were turned over to "special service" guards who administered their punishments. These were cruel, sadistic men without one iota of mercy or compassion. Those few people who survived later confided some of the horrors they experienced and witnessed.

Chanla learned that some were tied up, elbows tightly bound behind them, and chained to trees for days without food or water. Others were crucified in various unspeakable ways. Some were tied to tree limbs with slow-burning fires built under them. Some were beaten senseless, and still others had their wrists and ankles cut and were left to bleed to death. Sometimes the guards would bind a group together and place them in a thatched hut, which would then be set on fire. Many who survived the torture were sealed into caves and left to starve.

Women prisoners were special objects of sadistic torture. Small children would be pulled from mothers, swung in the air, and bashed against a tree or rock. Babies would be torn limb from limb. The little bodies would be hung from trees or poles to blacken in the sun like trophies.

While women also experienced the punishments inflicted on the men, special tortures were reserved for them. Bamboo stakes were thrust between their legs and up into their bodies. Their breasts would be amputated, and poisonous ants and other insects set on them. Pregnant women were often staked out, their bellies sliced open, and their babies taken and strung up by the neck or feet. The mothers would be left to bleed to death. Sometimes their livers, a delicacy to the Khmer Rouge, would be removed and eaten. Others had wooden stakes driven through their hearts.

Every conceivable horror was practiced on the helpless Cambodian people. The torturous treatment was unrelenting, devilish. Chanla prayed to God for mercy and deliverance. So far, Panno and Chanla had been spared the "prison experience," probably because they told the truth from the beginning, worked hard, were submissive and obedient, kept their mouths shut, and were careful not to annoy or irritate their captors or fellow villagers. But there was no assurance of what the next day would bring. Chanla frequently felt an almost physical angelic presence. He recalled the promise about angels of the Lord encamping around those who trusted Him.

Chanla determined that the family would escape this living hell as quickly as possible. Surely, even the violent Vietnamese would have more compassion than Chanla's fanatic fellow countrymen.

About this time the Khmer Rouge announced that a large reservoir would be built to provide irrigation for the area. With harvest nearly over, almost all the Group I work crews, including Chanla, were commandeered for this new project. As the excavation progressed, rumors circulated that it was actually to be a mass burial site for the people the Khmer Rouge were planning to kill. Many people had already died. The village was full of widows and orphans. Chanla's forebodings grew. He began earnestly praying for a way across the border.

One week later, like a thunderbolt from the sky, the opportunity came.

The explosion shook the ground so hard that a piece of roofing fell, narrowly missing Chanla. He sat up on his mat, peering around. Lack of nutrients in his diet for nearly two years made it almost impossible for him to see in the dark.

"Chanla, are you all right?" Panno called.

A second explosion rocked the house, and several things fell to the floor. Someone struck a match.

"Son, what is happening?" Mother's anxious voice reached his ear.

"It sounds like we're under attack. The supervisors at the reservoir seemed very distracted yesterday. I suspect it's the Vietnamese."

It was November 1977. Harvest was over, and Chanla had been working on the reservoir less than two kilometers away. He had been allowed to come home to sleep.

Chanla and Panno cautiously went outside. In the predawn light, they sensed a lot of movement around them. As the sky grew lighter, men with red headbands, the Khmer Rouge, scurried past, moving in jerking, darting fashion, apparently maneuvering to avoid bullets. It was difficult to know for sure which way they were going.

Other villagers crept carefully out of the buildings, trying to understand the situation. The mortar fire continued. Chanla and Panno guided their family to a nearby stand of trees, where they all lay flat on their stomachs.

Confusion was everywhere. Some of the Khmer Rouge were trying to fire at the invaders coming from the east, while others ran about the village ordering the people to evacuate to the west. The gunfire became almost constant, punctuated by exploding shells. No one knew what to do or which way to run.

By midmorning, the shelling had increased, and Chanla could make out the green uniforms of the advancing army. The soldiers had red stars on their caps and carried AK-47 assault rifles. They were Vietnamese. The Khmer Rouge were being pushed back. Salvation was on its way!

Most of the villagers clung to the ground or stayed inside their huts, fearing to move, lest they get caught in the cross fire. The Khmer Rouge were retreating, but few of the villagers went with them. It was as if they had held a silent election and a general consensus had been reached. The villagers would take their chances with the Vietnamese.

As the Khmer Rouge retreated, some of the villagers began running toward the advancing army, waving white pieces of cloth. Very quickly the rest followed, including

Chanla, his mother and the rest of his family.

The battle raged on, and shells fell all around them. But the momentum continued as hundreds of men, women, and children rushed toward the invaders. One shell exploded just ahead of Panno and Pitura, knocking them to the ground. Ears ringing and stunned, they lay still a few moments, then got up and continued running. Chanla felt as if they were moving in a dream. Bullets were whizzing all around them; shells were exploding; and many villagers fell, some killed, others seriously hurt. But Chanla's family of nine emerged untouched. He felt sure that angels were guarding them.

"Thank You, God," he prayed as they pressed on.

When they reached the Vietnamese encampment, soldiers partially surrounded the group. They quickly separated out the boys and men of military age and ordered them into a large house. They were tied up with long ropes, hands behind them, thirty men to a rope.

After securing the men and posting guards, the soldiers went back outside and ordered the women, children, and old people to "go home." With tears streaming down their faces, the villagers begged the Vietnamese for pity and protection from the Khmer Rouge. The soldiers shoved guns at their chests and yelled at them to leave quickly, or they would be forced to shoot them right there.

The people stayed as long as they dared, but the Vietnamese were unrelenting. Slowly they began retracing their steps toward the village. A few soldiers followed, waving guns, making sure they kept moving.

Tightly bound inside the building, Chanla witnessed the whole scene through an open window. He saw his mother and sisters shoved about and threatened. He saw Piteak intervene and pull them back. He witnessed their panic and despair. Never had he felt so utterly helpless!

Reality hit Chanla hard. The Vietnamese had not come to deliver the suffering peasants, but had come to reclaim "their land."

As for the prisoners, however, the Vietnamese had other plans.

Chapter 10
War Slaves

The Vietnamese captain strode into the room and looked at the men. "Khmer spies, murderers!" he shouted through an interpreter as he tromped about. "We ought to shoot all of you!" After a while, however, he and some of the other officers began interrogating the men, endeavoring to identify actual Khmer Rouge.

As the hours passed, sweat dripped and ran in rivers down the bodies of the men. They found it difficult to breathe in the small, hot room. Every now and then, one of the interrogators would shout, "Spies! They're all spies. Let's burn the place down!" Chanla wondered if they might really carry out their threats. He finally decided they were just bluffing.

It was easy to tell which prisoners were Khmer Rouge, thought Chanla, although they had removed their telltale red scarves. In contrast to the peasants, the Khmer Rouge appeared well fed and healthy looking. Although their faces bore no expression, a cool arrogance shone in their eyes. It was difficult for them to walk without a slight swagger. The Vietnamese, however, seemed unaware of these differences.

Chanla heard the sound of trucks pulling up outside, and shortly the men were packed into them. The trucks were large, but there were only two of them for nearly 200 prisoners. They stood pressed together, body against body, scarcely able to breathe.

91

As they were driven toward Vietnam, Chanla watched the continuing border fighting. Scattered bodies of both Vietnamese and Khmer Rouge soldiers lay along the roadsides. Sporadic shooting and mortar shells occasionally burst around them.

In the late afternoon, the prisoners arrived at a detention center, where they joined about 150 others. Interrogations continued. None of the prisoners had had any food or water that day. The weather was humid and suffocating. Finally, food arrived. A small dish of rice and a cup of water were placed on the ground in front of each prisoner. Chanla thought he had long ago lost any sense of dignity he once might have had. But now, humiliation was complete. His hands tied behind his back, the only way to eat the food and drink the water was to kneel down and lap it up like a dog. Their captors thought this was great fun to watch and laughed heartily.

Around 9:00 p.m. the prisoners were loaded back into trucks. The vehicles were less crowded this time, and the men could sit down and get some rest as they rode across the border into Vietnam.

Prisoners already crowded the jail by the time Chanla's group arrived, and the newcomers were ordered into the yard. They spent the rest of the night tied up, sitting on the ground in front of the jail.

Cooking began at dawn in a nearby market. Chanla could smell every herb and spice of the delicious-smelling food. He thought of the years they'd survived by eating watery rice gruel with a few vegetables and an occasional fish. The Khmer Rouge regularly killed village livestock, but the meat never reached the pots from which the villagers and laborers were fed.

The familiar aromas of oriental cooking reached Chanla. Tears formed in his eyes. He thought about his life in Phnom Penh and the meals Grandma and Mother had cooked. He couldn't remember ever being as hungry as he felt now. He buried his face in his shoulder.

"If they think we're Khmer Rouge soldiers," Panno said suddenly, "we'll be lucky to get out of this alive."

Chanla looked at him. "We'll die from hunger first."

By 11:00 a.m. the Vietnamese had rearranged the jail, and the doors opened to admit Chanla's group. Sixteen men were crowded into each small cell, which contained only a foul-smelling bucket for use as a toilet. Periodically the bucket was passed hand over hand and dumped out the window. The overwhelming stench made several men vomit.

Food finally arrived around noon and was delivered, one bowl for each cell for sixteen men. Surprisingly, the men took turns, each being careful to eat only his fair share. Chanla wasn't sure why, whether it was from fear of their captors, or some lingering respect for each other.

The soldiers continued bringing prisoners all day, until there were about 1,000 men at the prison.

By nightfall it was apparent that the prisoners didn't have room to sleep in the prison. Guards led the men to a large soccer field nearby and ordered them to lie on the damp, cold ground. None had a jacket or a blanket or even a bit of straw.

"Anyone who gets up and moves around or tries to escape will be shot," they were warned. Several tanks surrounded the group, as well as many guards. Chanla stretched out under the stars and found a flat rock for a pillow.

The following night, apparently delirious with fever and dehydration, one of the men suddenly stood up and began shouting.

"Get up! We must escape quickly. We are all to be killed at daybreak!" He began running, jumping over the bodies of the sleeping men. "Hurry up, hurry up," he urged loudly. "We must get back to our homeland before it is too late."

Half-asleep and dazed from their ordeal, a few of the men got up and began running.

"Stay down!" someone yelled. "The man is crazy."

"No! No! We'll all be killed," the crazed man insisted. "We must escape now."

Automatic gunfire began to spray over their heads. Shouts and screams pierced the air for a few minutes; then all was quiet. Eight bodies were recovered in the morning.

Food continued to be rationed at meager levels. Panno told Chanla that instead of executing them, the Vietnamese plan must be to starve them to death.

"We're still alive, brother. Just for today we should be thankful for that." But even Chanla began to worry.

On their sixth day of captivity, Chanla came down with malaria. As he alternately shook with chills and burned with fever, Panno begged the guards vainly for water and a blanket. They were still sleeping on the soccer field.

The next day, Chanla could neither eat nor sleep. Panno pleaded for medicine without success. That night it began raining. The prisoners pressed together for warmth and protection, but no one could sleep. The downpour became a flood, the water reaching knee level by morning. Everyone was extremely tired and thoroughly chilled.

During their period of suffering under the Khmer Rouge, Chanla had never felt so utterly dehumanized—like an animal—as he did during that first week of Vietnamese captivity. Each day the men were crammed into hot, stinking, standing-room-only cells. Each night they were herded back to sleep on bare, muddy ground in the open field.

One morning their group was ordered to line up and march to a waiting truck. Chanla could hardly stand, and Panno supported him as they made their way toward the vehicle. Chanla vomited with dry heaves every few feet. For the first time he felt he might truly be nearing death.

"Dear God," he prayed, "Father is gone. Preserve my life for the sake of the others."

Once on the truck, Chanla curled up in a corner. The vomiting stopped, giving him a measure of relief.

On the journey, the brothers noticed a great difference in the condition of the towns. They passed large apartment houses, busy factories, business offices, an airport, and a railroad station, all functioning and in good condition.

Panno squatted beside Chanla. "Brother, why has this Communist country escaped the fate of Cambodia? Our schools, hospitals, factories, and airports are in ruins. Our government workers and intellectuals have been killed." Panno's voice choked at this indirect reference to Father.

"I guess it is a different kind of Communist government," Chanla said weakly. "But I don't understand why they are so cruel to us."

As their truck lumbered through towns and villages, the people shook their fists and yelled, "Enemy, enemy!" At stop signs, some of the Vietnamese villagers jabbed sharp sticks through the truck railings, laughing as the prisoners cried out.

The trucks finally reached Long Khanh prison, located about eighty kilometers east of Ho Chi Minh City, formerly known as Saigon. About 4,000 prisoners were already there, a mixture of South Vietnamese, Khmer Rouge, and Cambodian peasants.

Chanla's group was like a herd of weary, smelly pigs. No one had bathed or changed clothes for over a week. They'd not had one good night's sleep. They looked and felt miserable and despondent.

Soon after arrival, blue prison clothes were issued, and prisoners were allowed to bathe. They lined up to eat, lined up to go to the toilet, lined up to wash, and sometimes had to take turns sleeping in the small spaces allotted. Chanla's health did not improve, and his depression deepened. He worried about Mother and the family, wondering if they had found safety. He feared he would never see them again.

Two days later, Chanla could not speak coherently and seemed to be in a coma. He was dimly aware of Panno bending over him and entreating God on his behalf. Panno begged the soldiers to help his brother. Finally, a nurse was sent, and Chanla was given an injection. Five hours later he showed improvement and was taken to the prison hospital.

Still Panno worried. As the days went by with no word, he feared Chanla might have died. If he did, would the Vietnamese tell him? He knew the Khmer Rouge would not. He continued to pray to Chanla's God and began looking for ways to escape the prison and reach the hospital. How much his older brother meant to him! Except for Panno's illnesses, they'd never been separated. He was greatly relieved when Chanla returned ten days later.

Weak, pale, and ravenously hungry, Chanla almost felt

like pinching the heads off the ever-present bedbugs and eating them.

The next day Panno picked up two spent shell casings on his way to the prison farm. When no one was looking, he managed to stuff two small potatoes into the casings, which he tucked into his belt under his shirt. With pounding hearts, Panno and Chanla ate their precious potatoes in the middle of the night. The next day a man was beaten and jailed for stealing a potato from the same garden.

During the month following their arrival at Long Khanh, the prisoners were gradually sorted out. Panno and Chanla were eventually assigned to Camp #11, which consisted mainly of peasant refugees.

Approximately 1,000 men were imprisoned in Camp #11. Divided into smaller work groups, they built roads, carried lumber from the forests, cut hay, dug wells, built houses, cleared brush, and planted rice and vegetables. In addition, they cleaned the prisons and the stool buckets.

Although rations improved somewhat, the prisoners were constantly hungry, and scavenged food wherever they could. Sometimes they would catch and eat small lizards and rodents. They stole edible greens and vegetables continually, especially potatoes.

Potatoes were particularly plentiful in this area, and the prisoners found many ingenious ways of obtaining them. At first they would secretly tuck them into their belts, under their shirts.

The Vietnamese caught on to this, but the guards were not allowed to strip-search or otherwise touch the bodies of the prisoners without provocation. So at night, as the men marched back from work to their barracks, they were ordered to lift their shirts. If potatoes were found in their belts, the men would be beaten or confined to a cramped jail cell, or forced to stand on hot rocks, handcuffed and shackled all day without food.

Prisoners began suspending the potatoes with pieces of cloth or string along their bodies inside their loose pajamalike pants. Some of the men managed to hide seven or eight potatoes at a time in this manner. This worked well for a while.

One day as Chanla's group returned from the field, they were lined up and commanded to "dance." The guards prodded them with rifle butts and bamboo sticks to keep them hopping. Nearly everyone's clothes began to shed potatoes, which rolled around on the ground. The spectacle was so funny that the guards began to laugh, and pretty soon everyone was laughing. With so many involved, it was difficult to determine just who was guilty. They were only threatened with harsh punishment if such a thing happened again.

Rather than giving up, however, the prisoners became more ingenious. They smuggled potatoes in garbage cans and in more secure areas of their clothes. One man was discovered with a potato hidden in a stool bucket. He was forced to eat it, unwashed, in front of his gleeful captors.

During the potato escapades, Chanla got into his first bout of serious trouble. His industrious and responsible ways led him to be promoted to captain of his group. During this time, some of Chanla's friends discovered that a portion of the prison fence had partly fallen. By putting a board over the barbed wire, they could climb across to the other side and reach the potato field. They did this for several nights with no problem at all, sharing their bounty with Chanla.

One night they persuaded Chanla to come along. "It's not fair for you to eat the potatoes and not take your turn getting them," said one.

"It's quite safe. We've not seen a guard there yet," said another. Chanla finally agreed to go.

Four of them slipped out late that night and crept to the fence. They climbed over it and vanished into the field. Chanla, the last, had reached the other side and taken only a few steps when he looked up into the face of a guard!

His captors wasted no time setting him up before the other prisoners and berating him for betraying their trust, and for his poor example. Chanla was embarrassed and humiliated. His comrades seemed able to flout rules at will, but Chanla's single attempt to get by with a small infraction netted him nothing but shame and punishment.

The Vietnamese had devised a rather unusual punishment. During the American presence in South Vietnam, many supplies had been shipped in large tin boxes, about six feet square. Prison officials took several of these, added a small door that could be tightly bolted, and cut a five- to six-inch square hole near the top to prevent suffocation. Men received sentences to solitary confinement in these boxes for varying periods of time, sometimes as long as two weeks. They went in with only the clothes they wore. Nothing was inside but a toilet bucket. With no blanket, lying on the tin at night was bitterly cold. In the heat of the day the box became an oven, and breathing was difficult. Prisoners sentenced for several days became delirious, and a few lost consciousness.

Because this was Chanla's first offense, and nothing had actually been stolen, he was sentenced to only twenty-four hours in the box. Chanla endured the misery, thanked God it wasn't worse, and wondered if he would be forever disgraced in the eyes of the Vietnamese. But in a few days, the incident was forgotten.

During these months as war slaves, Chanla, Panno, and the others walked ten to twenty kilometers a day to and from their work areas. Before and after work they lined up to be counted. The nightly indoctrination sessions were much like the ones under the Khmer Rouge, except there was a strong Soviet bias. The Vietnamese were supplied and supported by the Soviets. The Khmer Rouge, in 1975, threw off Vietnamese and Soviet domination and established a relationship with the Chinese.

While the Khmer Rouge brand of Communism was destructive and anti-intellectual, Vietnamese Communism did not go to these extremes. Educated people were humbled, stripped of most of their belongings, and paid a pittance of a salary, but usually remained in jobs commensurate with their abilities. Thus factories continued to run, cities were built, and progress did not entirely stop. As long as they demonstrated total, unquestioned obedience, the people had places to live and food to eat. Though they were watched, they were usually not punished as long as they conformed.

Prisoners however, found a different story. Tortures and mass executions stopped, but prisoners were worked mercilessly, starved constantly, and punished at the least provocation. Living conditions were primitive and deplorable.

As the months went by, Chanla fought depression. There seemed to be no hope of escape, and no end to his prison sentence. He missed his Bible. He wondered if Mother and the others were still alive.

His last glimpse of the family had been watching them scatter for cover as they were caught in the cross fire of the two armies. Had any of them been injured or killed? He wondered where they were. He continually prayed for them as well as for himself and Panno. Knowing that God was near brought comfort to Chanla's heart.

With a gift for languages, within a few weeks Chanla was speaking modest Vietnamese. About six months into Chanla's captivity, his superior discovered that Chanla not only understood Vietnamese but was also fluent in French, the second language in Vietnam. Within days, Chanla received the first promotion given to anyone in Camp #11. He became a translator for camp officials.

Popular with his new bosses, Chanla went everywhere with them. He learned a great deal about the Vietnamese Communist organization and the way its leaders thought and operated. Escape from the hard physical labor was also a welcomed relief. Chanla's food rations and general treatment improved, though he still returned to his cell to sleep at night.

Panno missed Chanla and continued working long, weary days with the other prisoners. His malaria and stomach cramps would return, periodically disabling him. Educated and bright, Panno also picked up the language quickly. In time he was assigned to a less demanding job—teaching Communist theory and ideology to the incoming prisoners!

In less than nine months, about 350 people died in Camp #11 from lack of sanitation, starvation, and untreated illnesses. Other prisoners quickly filled their places.

About this time, Chanla and Panno learned that their

captors were planning to recruit and train a New Khmer Army from among the prisoners. These soldiers were to fight along with the Vietnamese, helping to drive out the remaining forces of the Pol Pot regime and complete the liberation of Cambodia. As much as the brothers hated the cruel Khmer Rouge, the idea of fighting and killing their own Cambodian blood brothers shocked them.

Long Khanh Prison became the New Khmer Army training center, and the Vietnamese began drafting prisoners. Panno resisted, explaining that his continuing illnesses left him too weak to met the demands of army life. He was excused and allowed to continue teaching.

Meanwhile, Chanla joined a massive prison testing project. Among other things, his family background was intensively explored: father killed by the Khmer Rouge; no wife or children. His education and intelligence were tested. He was a high-school graduate who had started college, and his language fluency was already recognized.

One day Chanla was called into the prison administrator's office, where he met a Vietnamese general and his aide. The general spoke with him.

"Chanla, you have been chosen for a special work. It is a great honor. In your camp of 1,000 men, only two have been selected." He paused as Chanla attempted to absorb this information. The general then seemed to change the subject.

"Chanla, are you willing to drive a truck?"

What young man didn't long to drive a truck, especially the powerful vehicles of the Vietnamese army! Chanla felt a surge of excitement.

But years of discipline kept Chanla's emotions in check. After a pause, he spoke with deference.

"Yes, surely. I will be honored to drive for the People's Army."

"Good. Then it is settled. Prepare to be transferred north."

As he thought about breaking the news to Panno, Chanla had mixed feelings. His brother was recovering from another bout of illness, and Chanla did not want to cause him further distress.

But Panno had his own news.

"Chanla!" he exclaimed with enthusiasm. "I am being discharged from the army! I will leave in a month and will be assigned to work in a border village. I'm going to find Mother and the family!"

Chanla embraced his brother joyfully. "That's the best news yet! How I envy you." He looked down quickly, lest his brother read the anxiety in his eyes about his own fate.

Chapter 11
The Water Buffalo

The family numbly picked its way back over the littered road. How foolish they'd been to imagine the Vietnamese soldiers would help them!

"Mama, will we see our brothers again?" Pitura broke the silence.

Noting that Mother was beyond words, Grandma answered quickly. "Of course, Pitura, my child. They have made a terrible mistake. They think our boys are Khmer Rouge. They'll release them as soon as they discover their mistake."

Grandma sounded so confident that even Mother gathered courage from the possibility.

The family cautiously traveled back to the village, crawling much of the way to avoid bullets and mortar fire. Again, no one was hurt.

As they neared the village, Piteak edged up to Mother. He was fourteen now, and the man of what remained of the family. "Do you think it's a good idea just to walk back into the village? Khmer Rouge might be waiting to punish us or kill us for leaving."

Mother had recovered her perspective. "I really think they are too busy dealing with the invaders to worry about us right now," she answered. "But you're right. We should be careful."

"Piteak knows the area around the village better than anyone," Pitura offered. "Why don't we send him ahead to make sure the village is safe?"

It seemed like a good idea, so Mother reluctantly let him go.

Piteak crept silently through the trees and fields. He noted very little activity in the village. Except for a few other refugees straggling back, it seemed deserted.

Returning, Piteak escorted the family back to their home. The battle had moderately damaged the building, but the Khmer Rouge were gone and they saw no Vietnamese. Their possessions lay just as they had left them.

"Mama, I'm hungry," complained Chande, now four years old.

"Yes, Mama, we haven't eaten one bit of food all day," echoed six-year-old Vivatny. It was late afternoon.

Mother turned to Piteak and Prok. "Boys, run over to the communal kitchen and see what you can find. Be careful, though. There might be snipers about."

No one guarded the kitchen, and the storeroom door was open. Piteak picked up two cooking pots and filled them with rice and vegetables. Prok filled his arms with wood. Soon, Mother and Grandma had constructed a little stove and had their food cooking. For the first time in a great while, they did not go to bed hungry.

The night was crystal clear, and the moon shone full. Things seemed peaceful enough, but Mother knew it wouldn't last. She needed to quickly decide what to do. Did Chanla's God really have the power to help them, as Chanla said? She wondered if a God that powerful would be interested in their problems.

Gunshots and shells exploding in the distance provided the background for the restless sleep in the village that night. The freedom seemingly so close that morning was now farther away than ever.

In the morning, Piteak gazed out of the hut. The rising sun appeared larger and redder than he'd noticed before. A rooster's crow had awakened him minutes earlier.

Mother slipped over and sat down beside him. Her eyes were wet, and her heart was heavy. Piteak protectively put his arm around her.

"My son, we must begin moving toward Vietnam. That is

our best course now. We'll try to stay as close to Chanla and Panno as we can. Father may have been taken too."

"I'm sure you are right," Piteak said seriously. "At the moment, livestock are roaming the streets and everything is unguarded. But the Khmer Rouge will be back. They won't give up so easily."

After breakfast, Piteak, Pitura, and Prok left to see what they could find, while the rest began packing their possessions. Mother picked up the bundle of Father's things and held it tightly against her cheek.

"Try to bring back a cow or water buffalo," Grandma called after the boys.

Water buffalo were Piteak's specialty. In a few minutes he returned with a large black one. He tied it to a tree. Prok led a goat.

"Mother, there are no Khmer Rouge anywhere," he reported. "Two Vietnamese soldiers are playing cards at headquarters, but they don't seem to care what we do."

Pitura returned with two heavy baskets of food hanging from each end of a pole across her shoulders. She spotted the buffalo and goat. "Well, they've been telling us that the animals belong to the people," she laughed. "I guess it's about time the people got to use them."

Later, Piteak and Prok returned with a cart. They hitched the buffalo to the cart, and the family began loading it up.

On her next trip, Pitura brought a chicken and a basket of eggs. Piteak found a cow. They also found several cooking and eating utensils and some clothing. A jeep pulled up just at they finished packing. A Vietnamese soldier, by motions and some broken Cambodian, warned them to hurry. The Vietnamese were pulling back, and the Khmer Rouge would return shortly.

With their newly acquired wealth, the family quickly ventured onto the road, Piteak leading the buffalo, and Prok with the cow and goat. Several families took up the road ahead of them, and more were coming. All were loaded with as many bundles and baskets as they could carry; most had livestock as well.

As the family walked eastward along the dirt road,

several retreating Vietnamese soldiers passed them. Unlike the unpredictable Khmer Rouge, the soldiers' actions seemed well disciplined and controlled. Could it be that the quick surge across the border, followed by a retreat, was part of God's plan to help them escape? Mother reflected on the events of the past two days.

A mortar shell suddenly exploded just off the road, to their left. The water buffalo broke free of the cart and headed across a field. Piteak ran after him.

"Stop," called Mother. "Come back!" But Piteak, not about to lose his prize, kept running. Prok's animals also escaped, going in different directions. Mother lifted Chande from the cart, grabbed Prok's hand, and ran after Piteak.

Another shell exploded, cutting off the rest of the caravan. Grandma grabbed Vivatny and Pitura, and they lay flat on the ground. The retreating Vietnamese stopped and began returning fire. An intense shootout started.

"Stop, you stupid buffalo!" yelled Piteak. He caught the animal and sank to the ground behind it, holding the rope tightly. Mother, Prok, and Chande had followed a short way, then dropped to the ground when the battle started. Mother covered little Chande with her own body. Eleven-year-old Prok lay close beside her.

As the shooting lessened, Grandma, Pitura, and Vivatny, cut off from the others, spotted a dilapidated hut and decided to seek shelter there. Pitura warily opened the door.

"Grandma, someone is here." They waited a moment for their eyes to adjust to the darkened interior. "Look, it's an old lady."

She lay on a mat spread on the floor. The old woman looked at the strangers and tried to speak, but couldn't.

Grandma knelt by the woman, inspecting her more closely. "She's ill and very old and probably had to be left behind."

The old woman's plight distracted them from their own danger and the battle outside. Grandma rubbed her stiff limbs, speaking gently to her. Vivatny spooned water into her mouth, while Pitura looked for some food. The old woman drifted off to sleep.

As she became more aware of the battle outside, Pitura

worried about her mother and brothers.

"When I last saw them, they were chasing that big buffalo," Grandma said. "If they catch him, I'm sure they'll be safe hiding behind him."

Pitura smiled in spite of herself. With such a unique sense of humor, Grandma always knew how to break the tension. Still, Pitura was concerned. She thought about Chanla and Panno and wondered what had happened to them. She felt compassion for the abandoned old woman. What more could they do for her?

Pitura remembered how Chanla had prayed in times of perplexity and trouble. It always helped the family feel safer and less alone.

Pitura held the old woman's hand and reached for Grandma with her other hand. They bowed their heads.

"Supreme heavenly Ruler who is worshiped by elder brother Chanla, we ask You now to take care of us, Mother and our brothers, and this old lady." Pitura could go no further.

"That was a good prayer," Grandma said, biting her lip.

After about an hour, the shooting stopped, and Piteak could no longer see soldiers. He crawled across the field, pulling the frightened animal behind him. Eventually he reached Mother, Prok, and Chande, and they went back to the road. Their cart was still there, but the other animals had disappeared. Looking around for Grandma and the girls, Mother noted the hut and went to investigate. Piteak struggled to reconnect the buffalo to the cart.

Mother found the three sitting by the old lady. "She's dead," Pitura said softly. Grandma covered her with a tattered piece of blanket, and they went back to Piteak.

As their little caravan started up again, they passed several bodies—some soldiers, some refugees, and several animals. From long practice, the family steeled their emotions against the pain and suffering that could so easily overwhelm them. Fortunately, for the next few hours all of their attention was absorbed in keeping their family together and their caravan moving.

By nightfall they reached a small village lying mostly in ruins. The smell of death was again around them, and they covered their faces as best they could.

That evening Piteak drew water from a nearby well for the family and their buffalo. Though the water tasted strange, they were thirsty and tired, so no one complained.

The next morning Piteak went to the well for more water. As he dropped the bucket, he noted objects floating below. His eyes adjusted to the darkness inside the well, and then he saw the bobbing heads of three corpses. He felt sick. Mother noticed that he did not eat breakfast, nor did he bring water, but she said nothing.

For the next few days, the family traveled from one village to another, feeling extremely thankful for the buffalo and cart. From what they could learn, the Vietnamese Tang Chu Refugee Camp was the camp closest to where they thought Chanla and Panno were probably imprisoned.

When they reached Tang Chu, they were allowed to enter and were assigned a small space. The camp was located in the forest, and the refugees had to build their own shelters. Some men who were already settled helped Piteak, Pitura, and Prok build a shelter for their family. It had a roof but no walls. By putting their cart on one side and piling wood and branches around the other sides, they gained some privacy and protection. They were allowed to keep their buffalo.

The Vietnamese boss of this refugee camp gave each healthy adult nine kilograms (about twenty pounds) of food per month: one-third of it rice, one-third corn, and one-third flour. Children and those who were sick got one-third less rations, and the old and handicapped got two-thirds less rations. They soon discovered that this wasn't enough. The family learned to cut bamboo and weave baskets and make other useful attractive items that they could barter for additional food from surrounding villages.

Refugees on the Cambodian-Vietnamese border were required to work hard. They made roads and cleared forests, tended gardens and farmed bean fields, planted and harvested rice, and cut wood and made charcoal.

Mother found a great-uncle living in Ban Sang Camp and obtained permission to move there. Living conditions were better; the Vietnamese there had built rows of small houses from mud and thatch. The united families felt more secure, and less lonely and isolated.

During 1978, the border camps received aid from the Red Cross and several other international agencies. To the refugees, however, it soon became apparent that they were not in friendly territory. The relief agents were welcomed to the camps, where they generously distributed supplies. When the distribution was finished and the representatives had left, however, the Vietnamese collected everything of value that had been given to the refugees.

Ban Sang Camp was considered a model refugee camp, and visitors from the United States, Western Europe, and the Soviet Union flocked to see it. Groups of journalists also arrived occasionally, taking photographs and reporting on conditions to the outside world.

What these people didn't realize was that their visits were tightly controlled. Because visitors applied for permits in advance, the village was always warned. Refugees were thoroughly briefed on how to act and what to say. By threats of punishment, jail, exile, and even death, refugees were forbidden to tell the truth.

Shortly before the guests arrived, truckloads of rice, milk, medicines, clothes, pots and pans, blankets, and mosquito nets were distributed to the villagers for them to display for the visitors. After the pictures were taken, the reports filed, and the visitors gone, these things were collected and hauled away. The villagers could keep nothing.

This charade was repeated many times while the Dok family was there. In truth, the refugees were tired, ragged, and chronically hungry. They longed to tell the rest of the world the truth, that they were *not* receiving the generous supplies so kindly sent. Someone, somewhere, should know what was actually happening!

Despite the hardships during these months, Mother systematically visited prisons, hospitals, and work camps, looking for her sons and for Father.

Late one September day, Mother looked out the front door of her hut. Someone approached, smiling broadly. Her heart almost stopped. *It was Panno!*

It had been nine long months.

Chapter 12
The Secret Service

The day Chanla was to leave Long Khanh Prison, he was issued fresh clothes and given an army haircut. He went to say goodbye to his Vietnamese camp commander.

"I'm going to miss you, Chanla," he said, putting a hand on Chanla's shoulder. "You've been an excellent worker, and a good friend."

"I feel honored to be chosen for this mission," Chanla replied respectfully in French, still having no idea what his new mission was. A Cambodian driver for the Vietnamese army? A puzzling twist. The location of the assignment was also a mystery.

Arriving at the new camp the next day, Chanla met about seventy other hand-picked Cambodians who had been selected from the 8,000 men held in Vietnamese prisons. They were all sent to the hospital for health examinations.

This was no driving school, although Chanla did learn to drive. The badge on his uniform stated "Special Team Force, Division 0752." Chanla soon discovered the group had been chosen for training in the Vietnamese Secret Service, an elite army corps. The Vietnamese were still fighting the Khmer Rouge in Cambodia and had decided that some highly trained Cambodian secret service officers who knew the country, the language, and the people would be an asset to them. These men were considered the best.

For two months Chanla trained intensively in the ways of war. He learned how to enter an armed camp alone and how to sabotage an entire enemy installation with a few pounds of plastic explosives. He became expert at martial arts, and with different kinds of artillery. He made the highest grade of the group in his classwork and became the best shot in rifle practice. He was also popular with the Vietnamese teachers.

Chanla's living conditions changed dramatically. He wore the neat, well-made uniform of the Vietnamese army. He had comfortable quarters in the barracks, time to rest, and, best of all, plenty of good food to eat. He developed a solid, muscular body, and a healthy glow returned to his skin. The only difference he could note between the Cambodian group and the regular Vietnamese trainees was that he and his countrymen were constantly, though discreetly, watched.

After two months, the original group of seventy was narrowed down to fifteen men, and Chanla was appointed their leader. The others were sent to the front lines in various leadership positions with the New Khmer Army.

Those that remained in the small group were known as "second-level trainees," and life for them became even better. They enjoyed as much freedom as their Vietnamese counterparts. The strict surveillance stopped. They developed close relationships with their commander, his assistant, and the other officers who taught them, as well as each other. Graduation from level two assured placement in a high army position.

In the evenings, beautiful Vietnamese girls from nearby towns came to the training center to entertain the young men and dance with them. Their trainers hoped that these chosen young Cambodians, so long deprived of female company, would fall in love with and eventually marry Vietnamese girls. Thus, they would become more closely attached to their new country, and their loyalties would be more assured.

These were heady days for a young man of twenty-one who had spent three long years as a prisoner and war slave. But Chanla's thoughts were elsewhere. Three young

Cambodian women had been brought in from the border refugee camps to work as cooks in the officers' mess hall where Chanla ate his meals. All three were intelligent, attractive, and personable. But one in particular attracted Chanla's attention.

He noticed her the first day of his arrival. She was surely the prettiest, most graceful young woman he had ever seen. She had a wonderful smile. She completely captivated his thoughts. He couldn't wait for mealtime, and he would walk as close to her serving table as he could. She would smile shyly at him, but he was not sure how interested she was. Her name was Vandy Kim.

One evening at dinner she casually dropped a note on Chanla's tray. His heart did double time as he tucked it into his pocket. He opened it as soon as he was alone.

"Esteemed sir," it read. "Would you like to meet me by the water fountain at eight o'clock tonight?"

Would he! He was there waiting when she arrived, and he was not disappointed. She was as sweet, gentle, and kind as she was lovely. The noisy parties indoors no longer attracted Chanla. He and Vandy met as often as they could, and got to know each other as they walked and talked in the balmy evenings under the stars.

Born in Battambang province in western Cambodia, Vandy Kim was the fourteenth of fifteen children. Her parents worked hard to provide for the large family. Her oldest sister had gone to school and received a good education; then she had married an army officer and moved to the capital, Phnom Penh.

As the older children grew up, schooling became less and less possible. Vandy's mother especially worried about her smallest daughter, who was exceptionally bright. She arranged for Vandy to live in Phnom Penh with her married sister. Schools were plentiful there, and Mother felt sure that Sister would look after Vandy's education.

Vandy arrived at her sister's when she was ten years old. Thoughts of schooling quickly vanished when she was told she was responsible for the couple's two small children. Her stern brother-in-law, an officer in President Lon Nol's army, wanted his "educated wife" to take a well-paying job in government. Soon Vandy realized she was no more than a convenient and inexpensive servant to the family. She resented this betrayal and tried to get word to her mother.

That task proved formidable. She was rarely taken anywhere, so she was unable to learn her way around the city. When visitors came, Vandy was carefully watched. One day she found her way to an uncle's house, but just as she got there, her brother-in-law drove by. He spotted her, took her home, and punished her severely.

Vandy was sixteen when the Khmer Rouge overthrew the Lon Nol regime. Most of the military were executed immediately, including her brother-in-law and his family. Vandy escaped from the city with friends during the exodus. They eventually reached a village near the border of Vietnam.

Hard work was not new to Vandy, and she quickly learned to fit into the new order of things. She was drafted along with other young people into the Productivity Army and lived in labor camps. She was respectful, responsible, and well liked.

By the time Vandy reached the Vietnamese refugee camp, she was skilled in survival and had developed considerable inner strength and independence. Her competent work and her shy friendliness attracted the notice of the Vietnamese, who recruited her to work in their army training camps.

Despite her hard life, Vandy retained a soft femininity and a gentle spirit. Chanla lived for their evening walks. Her unselfish devotion and love warmed and comforted him. He couldn't remember being so happy. Vandy Kim was everything he had ever dreamed of.

Chanla's superiors smiled and tolerated the friendship. Chanla was a favorite, and it was easy to indulge him. Besides, they knew it would soon be over.

Precisely to avoid such attachments, the Cambodian girls were placed on a rotation basis through the different camps. The leaders knew that Vandy's rotation would soon end and she would be gone. They felt certain Chanla's infatuation would pass.

As the time neared for Vandy to move on, protective Chanla wanted her out of the Vietnamese system and back at the refugee camp. During her last few days of duty, she feigned illness and begged for a leave of absence. Her superiors approved the idea, supposing that she would be farther away from Chanla.

Parting was difficult. Vandy promised to find his family and to send him messages. Chanla pledged his love and bade her a tender farewell.

A few days later, Chanla was called to the Training Center's lobby and was surprised to find his mother there. It had been so long, he had sometimes felt he would never see her again.

"I have looked many months for you in three provinces," she told him. "Now I have found you. Panno is with us in Ban Sang Camp—and so is Vandy Kim." Mother watched her son's face as she said the girl's name.

Chanla's eyes lighted up, and the look on his face answered her question. After six weeks of almost nightly meetings, Chanla missed Vandy terribly. But he was glad she had found his family.

"Mother, isn't she a wonderful girl? I'm sure you'll love her. I want to marry her."

But Mother had other things on her mind. "My dear son, you must leave this place. War is insane. You must not join this madness and get yourself killed. Is it not enough that Father and Reni are gone?"

Chanla didn't answer, but grasped Mother's hands. He had become increasingly disturbed about his involvement in the sophisticated Vietnamese war machine. It did not seem right that he should become a secret agent for an oppressive government. At length he promised Mother he would look for an opportunity to escape, but cautioned her to tell no one.

Chanla bade his mother goodbye, thanking God that she and the other family members were safe and well.

His training now took another turn. During their fourth month, Chanla's group received heavy Communist indoctrination. He had to accept that the Vietnamese followed the same Communist ideology he had determined to leave behind. "The party" was everything. Religion and personal rights were not respected, and the people were required to render uncomplaining, submissive service according to the will of their leaders. It was also obvious that tiny, crowded Vietnam with its twenty-two million people coveted fertile, sparsely populated Cambodia.

Chanla's mind was in turmoil. For the first time in years, he was free from physical suffering. He had plenty to eat, and he had the respect of his superiors and his fellow students. He had the opportunity to be an important military leader of the future.

Chanla prayed. He did not have his Bible, but he thought of Moses, Daniel, Esther, and Paul. None of them had allowed honor and high positions to compromise their service to God and their dedication to doing what was right. Chanla could not reconcile his present life and activities with God's will for his life.

About two weeks later, Mother again visited Chanla, accompanied with Great-Uncle and Vandy Kim. Once more they urged him to escape. Mother and Great-Uncle soon left, but Vandy Kim stayed that evening. He was so overwhelmed at seeing her again that he asked her to marry him. She told him she would, but they must get out of this mess first.

Alone that night in his room, Chanla struggled with his thoughts. He pondered more about the *timing* than about the *decision*, which he had basically made. One of his classmates had tried to escape a few weeks before, but had been captured. As punishment his fingers had been shot off. What chance would Chanla have as a fugitive in a foreign country? The secret service had many ingenious ways of finding its men. Although Chanla felt loved by his superiors, could they forgive him this act? He decided to wait for a better time.

At nine o'clock the next morning, he changed his mind. It was Sunday, and he took a bus to the village market, a common practice for soldiers on free days. He met Vandy Kim at the bus station. They walked around the marketplace hand-in-hand, and she casually passed him a package of peasant clothes. Chanla found a private place and changed clothes. He disposed of his army trappings in a tall garbage can, then quickly walked to a nearby dock, where Vandy Kim had a boat ready and waiting.

Just as the boat started off, a group of soldiers ran onto the dock. They carefully scanned the place, but did not recognize Chanla and Vandy. The two had carefully busied themselves in the boat and kept their faces turned out, toward the water. Chanla knew that his superiors would quickly locate his family. He also suspected that Vandy Kim might be tortured if they found her and thought she knew his whereabouts. So when they reached the Cambodian side of the river, they headed for the forests, planning to keep hidden for the next few months. They soon found several other people in hiding and joined them. The group constantly changed locations for safety reasons.

Two days after Chanla's escape, his captain, the number-two man in the Vietnamese secret service training program, appeared at Mother's door with one of Chanla's classmates, a man named Bunna. He was courteous and friendly to the family. He told them that the officers knew of Chanla's love for Vandy Kim, and they believed this was his motivation in escaping.

Mother and the family could honestly tell them they had not seen Chanla or the girl, and had no idea where they might be. The captain told them that when Chanla turned up, they should assure him that all was forgiven and that he could safely return, marry Vandy Kim, and live near the army base.

Captain Oung Teur spent several more days personally looking for Chanla. But with thousands of Cambodian refugees of similar appearance milling through the border camps, they finally decided it was hopeless. The village leaders were instructed to watch Chanla's family, which they carefully did for the next few weeks.

Chanla's secret service training now came in handy. He knew how to build shelters that could hardly be seen, even when standing just a few feet away. He knew how to survive in the forests and jungles. He knew the ways Vietnamese soldiers organized their patrols to hunt people down. His hair grew out. Within a few weeks, dressed in shabby peasant clothes and crude sandals, he looked the same as the other refugees crowding the border camps.

Chanla worried about Vandy. He knew that accompanying a rough, roving group of hunted men was dangerous. His protective instincts recoiled at watching the hardships she endured, though Vandy herself remained cheerful and did not complain.

After about three weeks, he risked sending her home with a basket of berries, fruits, mushrooms, and greens that he had garnered from the forests. Vandy Kim was questioned, and she admitted having been with Chanla. However, she reported that he kept moving among the border refugees, staying at different locations each night. They accepted her story and did not abuse her. But they redoubled their watchful efforts, feeling sure Chanla would eventually try to slip home to see her and his family.

Chanla developed ingenious ways of sending baskets of fruit and other "presents" to his family. They would usually find them at their door in the morning. Inside would be a note from Chanla, reassuring them that he was well. After a time he suggested some furtive meetings, one person at a time, outside of camp. Chanla occasionally slipped into camp in the darkness of night. After all, he had been trained well in these kinds of tactics.

When the Communist Vietnamese army invaded Cambodia in November of 1977, they had begun along the common border of the two countries. This is why Chanla's village was one of the early ones to fall into their hands, and Chanla and Panno were among the first groups of prisoners to be taken. The Vietnamese were aware of the brutality and murderous practices of the Khmer Rouge. But life-long enmities between the two peoples persisted, and the Vietnamese did not wholly trust the Cambodian peasants to be loyal to them. They also didn't know how many Khmer Rouge were posing as innocent peasants.

For these reasons, the Vietnamese made prisoners of all able-bodied men and drove their families into tightly supervised refugee camps.

Although the purges and mass executions stopped, as

well as most of the tortures, the treatment was harsh, and people were severely punished for minor infractions. By keeping the refugees tired, weak, and constantly hungry, their new captors hoped to keep them submissive and obedient.

Similar tactics were used on the prisoners. They were kept hungry and weary, their quarters crowded and dirty, and they were regularly punished. In addition, their captors missed no opportunity to ridicule and humiliate them.

After weeks of this kind of treatment, when the men had literally lost their ability to even care about what happened to them, conditions began to improve. They were occasionally commended for their submissiveness and obedience, and sometimes even their work. Discipline became noticeably less severe, and food rations improved. Their captors told the prisoners they were proving themselves loyal, trustworthy men and expressed pleasure at the progress of their rehabilitation. In such a setting, the prisoners grasped at straws of hope and began to view their captors in a more favorable light.

The prisoners received regular news reports. Pol Pot and his mad cohorts continued their determined resistance against the Vietnamese. The unbelievable, senseless atrocities continued. By mid-1978, the Vietnamese controlled the eastern part of Cambodia, but Pol Pot's Khmer Rouge still held on to Phnom Penh and the western half of the country.

To increase their chances of success in Cambodia, the Vietnamese picked two men to head a Cambodian government-in-exile. Heng Samrin and Hun Sen were formerly Khmer Rouge, but they had not supported Pol Pot's murderous regime. They had repented and had shown a cooperative spirit toward the Vietnamese. Heng Samrin became the president, with Hun Sen as chief deputy of the fledgling People's Republic of Kampuchea, and the Vietnamese promised to help them drive out the remainder of the Pol Pot regime. Owing their survival and power to the Vietnamese, the men pledged cooperation.

As the "free Cambodians" and the Vietnamese gained strength, the Pol Pot regime experienced increasing difficulties. Many Khmer Rouge and civilians escaped into Vietnamese-occupied territory to join the resistance effort.

In August of 1978, the Vietnamese went through their prisons, enlisting Cambodians to join the New Khmer Army. It was during this time that Chanla was chosen for his special mission and sent north. Panno had also been chosen, but, he did not accept because of ill health. Panno continued for a few weeks as an instructor and was eventually discharged from service.

During his final weeks, Panno watched many "rehabilitated" Cambodian prisoners march off in new uniforms to serve as soldiers. They would do *anything* to get out of their present hellhole and possibly return to their own country. Many of them hated the Khmer Rouge and thirsted for revenge.

As the prison population dwindled, Panno's services were no longer needed, and he was assigned to work in the refugee camps. Due to the efficient organization and good records of the Vietnamese, he had been able to find his family and reunite with them.

Life in the refugee camp was a happy and welcome change for Panno, but it pained him to see the harsh conditions imposed on them. The discipline, rations, and regimentation were little different from prison life, though the people were allowed more freedom of movement and were permitted to live as families in simple, crude huts. Panno endeavored to fit in. He encouraged his family, trying to bolster their spirits and foster the flame of hope.

Shortly after Panno's arrival, the camps began a concerted effort to register as many refugees as possible in the New Khmer Army. Some were eager to join and fight the hated Pol Pot regime. But Panno and others knew that replacing one Communist government with another would not change things very much in the long run. Besides, they couldn't face the prospect of killing their own people, even if the reasons seemed legitimate.

Eventually enlistment became mandatory, and Panno's name was called. Panno explained his history of illness, and his discharge from the Long Khanh Training Center because of it. But Panno looked all right to them. He was accused of evading the army and not carrying his full workload, and was sentenced to jail, with hard labor.

Panno suffered a great deal during those days, and again prayed to Chanla's God for relief. A week later, he experienced a severe recurrence of his malaria. As Panno lay in his prison cell, alternately chilling and burning with fever, vomiting his food and moaning with severe cramps and dysentery, the official realized he had told the truth and sent him home.

On January 7, 1979, the Communist Vietnamese army and their ally, the New Khmer Army, succeeded in driving Pol Pot and the remnants of his army out of Cambodia. In the next few weeks, they completed occupation of the country. They formally installed Heng Samrin and Hun Sen as the puppet leaders of the new People's Republic of Kampuchea.

The refugees on the Vietnamese-Cambodian border were anxious to return to their homeland. About 20,000 of them milled about the border camps, waiting for permits, but the camp leaders seemed in no hurry. Finally, at the end of their patience, the people decided to take matters into their own hands. The message passed by grapevine up and down the border camps. On a certain date and time the refugees would leave for home, all together.

The night before, Chanla appeared and helped the family pack. They repaired their little cart but had to pull it themselves, as their buffalo had long since been commandeered. At the given time, the entire refugee population began moving west. Surprised and confused by the vast numbers of people, the guards fired shots over their heads, but did not otherwise oppose them. As they crossed into Cambodia, the people began singing and dancing in the roadways, hugging and congratulating each other. They were going home at last!

Their joyous outbursts were short-lived, however.

Chapter 13
Discovered

Something suddenly exploded in the middle of the road, and everyone instinctively dropped to the ground. But it was too late: two people were dead and several injured. Deadly bombs were hidden in little piles of bamboo along the road. A man cried out in agony; his foot was impaled on an iron spike.

The people quickly learned they were traversing a no-man's land between the two countries; a place where bitter battles had been fought. Not only was the area littered with land mines, traps, and bombs, but occasional Khmer Rouge guerrillas still roamed about, shooting at anyone who appeared to be coming from Vietnam. Several refugees were felled by their bullets.

Chanla and other young men who had been combat-trained walked ahead, searching for the deadly devices. They were able to clear the main road and keep it relatively safe. But despite repeated warnings, a few people continued to make occasional excursions off the main road to reach food or water, or to relieve themselves, resulting in more deaths and injuries.

After about a day, they began to pass villages and rice fields. The massive destruction before them filled them with sorrow and rage. Houses, schools, offices, stations, roads, and farms were either burned or blown up by bombs and mortar blasts. As the Khmer Rouge army retreated, they apparently decided to leave nothing of value to the invaders. Their once-lovely country had become a vast ruin.

A few peasants survived in the villages on small plots of land, and some of the refugees joined them. But the Dok family pressed on. They wanted to find their home village, where Father and Mother had been married and most of the children born. The Khmer Rouge had turned them away three and a half years ago, but now the Vietnamese soldiers told them they were free to go anywhere they wished.

It took the Dok family three weeks to reach Svay Rieng province and find their hometown. It had been a thriving city, the hub of the province, prosperous and beautiful. Now, it was scarcely recognizable. Much of it lay in ruins, and the people who remained were very poor. They located a few of their relatives and a handful of old friends. All had been plundered and exploited by the Khmer Rouge, and were now living on meager crops and scant rations.

The family found their former home. The once-neat brick courtyard was littered with rubble—pieces of brick and coal, and masses of weeds crawling with insects. The ruins of the house were partially overgrown by jungle. The well had been used as a garbage dump and smelled terrible.

The place that had been home was now a place of utter desolation. They looked a long while. It was near evening, and they walked back to the road, their hearts broken.

Chanla spoke first. "Mother, there's nothing for us here."

"I feel the same way, my son," Mother said. "This place can barely support the people who are already here. But what shall we do?"

"What about Phnom Penh? Our house might still be there!" Panno was the family optimist.

"Maybe so, maybe not," put in the usually cheerful Grandma. "But it could be a lot easier in the city for people like us. And it would be the best place to look for Father." Grandma knew that Mother had not given up hope of one day finding him.

Mother noticeably brightened. "I'd like to go, but it's a

long trip. We don't have a motorcycle, bicycle, or even a buffalo."

Chanla still had escape on his mind. Going to Phnom Penh would get them that much closer to the Thai border.

"Let's go," he said enthusiastically. "We did it once; we can do it again. The four of us men will take turns pulling the cart." He winked at Piteak and Prok, now fifteen and twelve. "Our family is tough. We can walk all the way if we have to."

And that is what happened. It was much like the exodus from Egypt. The Dok family slept in fields, remains of temples, and shells of buildings. Harvesttime was past, but many fields were scarcely touched. They gleaned rice and harvested edible plants and fruit along the way. The family began to talk freely again and to sing familiar songs. The children begged Mother and Grandma for stories of the past. Despite the hardships, life seemed almost normal again.

They were continuously shocked at the amount of devastation they passed. They worried whether anything would be left of the spacious, tree-lined city of Phnom Penh they had once known. It had been a true jewel of the Orient.

After several weeks of travel, they arrived in their beloved city. Chanla was amazed to find it almost intact. Their house was gone, and some areas consisted of rubble and ruin, but most of the city was much as they'd left it. During the exodus, the people had been forced to walk away from virtually everything they owned. Apparently when the Vietnamese troops arrived, there hadn't been much of a struggle either.

But the once-busy, thriving city looked desolate. Once nearly a million people had lived there, but during Pol Pot's rule the population had shrunk to 10,000. It became headquarters for the leaders, the military, and a few thousand civilians dragooned to serve the tyrannical regime. Although workers lived in the city, their families were sent to the countryside. Pol Pot barricaded all but two of the broad boulevards and destroyed most of the vehicles.

By the time Chanla and his family arrived, city dwellers who had been expelled nearly four years before were streaming back. A pitiful sight, they owned nothing except a few utensils and ragged clothes, which they carried suspended from poles across their shoulders. People moved into any apartment they could find, on a "first come, first served" basis.

Business and commerce were virtually destroyed, and only a few factories operated. Little food, few markets, and even fewer jobs existed. After viewing the pitiful remains of their home, the family felt too sad to stay.

Eventually they moved into an abandoned house in the nearby village of Chabar Ampoa. An empty plot of land lay next to the place, and Mother immediately purchased some seeds. She and Grandma had become experts in gardening, and soon every square centimeter of available land was planted.

Mother and the older children traveled around the countryside, trading some of their belongings for baskets of food and useful products made by the villagers. They carried these into the more prosperous parts of the city and traded them for items needed in the villages. In this way, going back and forth, day after day, they made small gains and gradually improved their living situation.

Chanla and Vandy Kim were anxious to get married, but Chanla was still in hiding. Besides, they knew of no clergy or even a functioning church. The couple decided to fashion their own wedding ceremony. Using Chanla's half Bible, in the presence of their family, Chanla and Vandy Kim pledged themselves to each other. Chanla prayed. That simple service symbolized their dedication to each other. Chanla found a little house close by, and the couple moved into a home of their own.

Shortly after this, Chanla risked a trip into the city. The chances of meeting anyone who knew him from Vietnam seemed remote. Even so, how could he be recognized among the masses of look-alike refugees, especially with his altered appearance? Chanla was still thinking escape to Thailand and wanted to look at maps and pick up information about how to get there.

As he walked down one of the boulevards he noticed a jeep approaching with a Vietnamese officer and driver. Chanla was petrified to recognize his old boss from the secret service, the number-two man, Captain Oung Teur. This was the same man who had personally hunted for him in the jungles of Vietnam five months before.

Chanla dropped his head, looking steadily at his feet, but he was too late. The jeep stopped and the captain jumped out.

"Hello, Chanla," a big voice boomed. "So you are here now. Where do you live?" His tone was friendly.

Chanla was so startled he couldn't speak. He tried to smile. The man noticed his peasant garb.

"Well, my boy, we have missed you. Would you like to join the new liberation army? We need men of your caliber." The captain betrayed no hint of hostility or vengeance. Chanla was dumbfounded.

"I—I have a large family to care for—and a new wife— "

"Well, well, congratulations! We can help you with that. Think it over. I'll see you in a few days." The captain returned to his jeep and continued on his way. Chanla couldn't believe what was happening. He expected to be taken prisoner, right there. Nevertheless, he was panic-stricken. Though the man was friendly and seemed sincere, Chanla did not trust him. How could a secret service soldier desert and not be punished?

As he ran back to the village, he thought of the experience of a friend of his, another of the "chosen fifteen." The man had been recognized and captured on the street of Phnom Penh about a month before. He was taken to the roof of government headquarters and forced to kneel, bound hand and foot, before a blood-spattered wall. As the firing squad cocked their guns, an officer rushed out and commanded them to wait. He proceeded to tell the man he was too valuable to die—it would be a great waste. The new Cambodian government needed men like him. If he would agree to work with them, they would spare his life. Thus blackmailed, he had entered into their service.

Chanla also thought of Vandy. Just that morning she had told him that she was pregnant. It had increased his determination to get out of Cambodia. He wanted his child to be born in freedom.

He raced to Mother's house first, breaking the news and seeking advice. Chanla's thought was to leave immediately for Thailand. Mother was frightened, too, and wanted to protect her son.

"I suppose we should all go," she said slowly, "but we need time to prepare. We don't know the way, and we're not familiar with that part of the country. Besides," she said, hesitating a moment. "We haven't had a chance to look for Father."

"And if we travel together we will be easy to find," added Panno. "We need to split up and meet near the border."

"Why don't you go to your home, Chanla, and hide there?" Mother finally suggested. "Hardly anyone knows that you and Vandy have moved. Vandy can stay with us, and we'll find a way to send you food."

Chanla agreed to this. When several days went by and nothing happened, he began to relax. He also got restless. He decided that he and Vandy, at least, should head for the border. That night he slipped back to Mother's house to talk over his plan.

Suddenly someone knocked. Chanla stepped to the back of the house, heading for the back door. But he noticed several soldiers stationed outside.

Mother opened the door and admitted a Vietnamese officer and his aide. He spoke in French. "We know this is Chanla's house, and we know he is here," he said, not unkindly. "We wish to talk to him."

Realizing escape was now out of the question; and true to his family code, Chanla stepped into the room without hesitation and looked directly at the officer. "I am Chanla, and I am ready to go with you," he said in a firm voice. He turned toward his family, bowed slightly, and told them not to worry about him. He accompanied his captors to their jeep, praying fervently all the way to Phnom Penh.

This time the execution scenario was dispensed with. He was escorted directly into the office of Captain Oung Teur, who dismissed the others and invited Chanla to be seated.

"Chanla, you were our best student at Division 0752

training camp. We had big plans for you." The man's voice was friendly and sincere. "We all liked you and trusted you. You did a bad thing when you ran away from us, but we knew you were in love. You were also worried about your family. We can forgive you for these things."

Chanla looked into his old teacher's eyes and smiled weakly. "You are more than generous, sir. I do not deserve such kindness."

"You can escape Vietnam, my friend," the captain continued, "but you cannot escape Cambodia. This is your country. We are trying to help your people rebuild it. We need capable, trustworthy men like you."

Despite the kindly approach, Chanla remained tense. What was coming next?

"We have an extraordinarily fine position to offer you. This new government needs a good intelligence department, and we cannot think of anyone more capable and responsible to put in charge of it than you. You would work directly under President Heng Samrin (the new Cambodian leader) and Hun Sen, his chief administrative officer. Besides that, you would report to only one Vietnamese officer, who would be me. Chanla, are you willing to help us?"

The offer was unbelievable. From hunted refugee to chief of Cambodian intelligence? The offer was also overwhelming. So much power for so young a man! It took a while for Chanla to comprehend the impact of the position he had been chosen to assume. But other thoughts rushed through his mind as well. What if he refused? Would he be allowed to live? He knew too much, and they would not be able to trust him. He saw no real choice, no way out.

Chanla bowed slightly. "I am greatly honored by your most generous offer. I am ready to begin immediately."

"Good, good!" exclaimed the captain heartily. He stood, shook Chanla's hand, and slapped him on the back. "You will not regret this decision." They drank a toast to the new "free" Cambodia.

The next day he was fitted with a Vietnamese officer's uniform, shiny black boots, and insignias indicating his office and rank. As Chanla walked about with the captain and was introduced to officials, bosses, associates, and subordinates, he received respectful salutes and near-reverential treatment. He thought how Daniel must have felt when he was elevated from a war prisoner to the chief of Babylon's wise men, and later to prime minister. He determined to remain humble like Daniel, and as loyal to his God.

As Chanla became more familiar with his job requirements, he realized that the Vietnamese were not entirely trustful of the puppet government they had set up. They needed an agent, a kind of in-house "mole," to keep them informed of what was going on. Chanla was a man they knew well. He was honest, and they felt their generosity toward him would gain his loyalty. As a cover, he was to work under the new premier, with the mayor of Phnom Penh as his immediate supervisor. He was also to train other Cambodian agents much as he had been trained in Vietnam.

The next few days proved intriguing as Chanla was introduced to the workings of the new "free" Cambodian government. Some of his associates were former classmates from the Division 0752 school. Two of them had already been installed as heads of different branches of the government. Nearly all the educated people of Cambodia had either been killed or escaped the country, so the few left, especially those known by the Vietnamese, had opportunities for rapid advancement. The future for Chanla looked bright indeed.

The captain sent a messenger to inform the family that Chanla was safe but would be detained a few days. Distrustful of Communist promises, Mother, Panno, and Vandy continued to worry. Detention usually meant one thing: imprisonment and probable execution. Because of Chanla's desertion, he might also be tortured.

At week's end, Chanla was driven back to his family in a military vehicle. At first they did not recognize this imposing officer in his fine uniform. When they finally realized it was Chanla, the older ones began to cry, and the younger ones whooped with joy.

Chanla suspected that he was being watched, but he

had no desire to escape. He felt valued, needed, important. He was certain he could find many ways to help his countrymen. Surely God had prepared him for such a time as this!

Chanla soon realized that no one had any real authority over him. Although the premier and his administrative assistant were technically his bosses, they knew little about intelligence work and left him relatively free to do as he wished. He and the mayor became good friends and worked in an atmosphere of trust. His Vietnamese boss had no reliable way to cross-check his reports and accepted them with few questions. Chanla reported the good things about his Cambodian brothers, throwing in an occasional report of a small misdemeanor to avert suspicion.

The more he fully realized the power and authority he had, the better Chanla felt. He believed he would be able to make a valuable contribution toward rebuilding his country and regaining its freedom.

But he saw many other things as well. One day he visited the school where his father had taught. As with several of the other school buildings in the city, the Khmer Rouge had turned it into a prison, complete with torture chambers, records of people's names, and their dates of execution. Underground rooms were full of bones and skulls.

Although the Vietnamese turned these places into museums and monuments to the atrocities of the former regime, Chanla learned that the military were still arresting people secretly at night. Most of them were accused of being Pol Pot's men or of being connected to a resistance movement. There were no trials, no justice for these men. They were either executed the same night or shipped to Ho Chi Minh City or Hanoi, to be dealt with there.

Large warehouses in Phnom Penh were filled with the wealth that the Pol Pot regime had taken from the people. Most of this was shipped to Vietnam, although a portion was reserved for the Cambodian people. Symbolic distributions were made from time to time, especially when journalists and foreigners visited the city.

Food became increasingly scarce. During the war many of the crops had either been destroyed or left rotting in the fields. Planting had been neglected. Farmers feared to enter their rice fields because mines and booby traps had been planted in some of them.

The new government began reorganizing the people, assigning them to work groups and imposing quotas. Cambodians were required to obtain permits to travel from place to place. Their newfound liberties gradually eroded as the heel of Communism once again ground down upon them.

Hospitals and clinics reopened, but less than ten percent of Cambodia's doctors and nurses had survived Pol Pot's purges. Although relief agencies and volunteers came to help, medical care in general was atrocious. Little medicine was available, and extreme means were frequently used to treat relatively simple problems.

People flocked to the hospitals with infected wounds and open fractures. If a person had an infected finger, he often got his hand amputated. A toe wound frequently resulted in a foot amputation. Because of the lack of antibiotics and sterile techniques, many people died and others emerged crippled for life. Often diseases were misdiagnosed, and the wrong treatment was given.

Things continued to get worse. Chanla soon realized that Cambodian president Heng Samrin had little power. He existed to convince the outside world that the Cambodians were developing their own government. In reality he was a helpless puppet, manipulated by the Vietnamese to shape the country to their plans.

Large quantities of food, medicine, and other supplies arrived from the outside world for the relief of the hungry, suffering people. But as before, as soon as the pictures were taken, the news reports filed, and the benefactors had left, the Vietnamese seized most of these things either for themselves or to send back to Vietnam. Chanla grew increasingly disillusioned and discouraged as he realized his own helplessness in the face of such overwhelming odds. He began thinking again of escape—and freedom.

During this time, Chanla searched through the records of the labor camps, prison camps, and hospitals of the previous regime. Day after day he searched for the name "Whirling Cloud Camp," the last known location of his father. One weekend as the family sat around eating supper, Chanla told Mother of his efforts.

"Mother, I've spent days searching through old Khmer Rouge records, trying to find information about Father. Great-Uncle heard that he was being sent to Whirling Cloud Camp. Panno and I have been searching for this camp for over two years and have found nothing. No one has heard of it! Now I've searched the records at headquarters, and still find no trace of it. Great-Uncle must have been mistaken in his information."

Piteak's face became ashen. He tried to speak, but made only a strange noise. The whole family looked at him, startled.

"Piteak, what is the matter?" Mother cried. "You are white as a ghost."

Piteak found his voice.

"Yes, there was a Whirling Cloud Camp, and I saw it with my own eyes. It was a death camp, where men were sent to be killed or to be worked without food and water until they died."

He choked up for a moment and could not go on. Stunned, the family sat in silence.

Piteak continued. "I told Mother about seeing two young men forced to dig their own graves. They were clubbed with rifle butts until they fell into the hole. The soldiers then buried them alive. It was so horrible, it made me sick. I still have nightmares about it."

Chanla checked the next day under "death camps" and found Whirling Cloud listed.

Mother became despondent. After a few days of wrestling with her grief, she told Chanla and Panno she was ready to leave the country whenever they found an opportunity.

Chanla, too, was ready to go. In all his dealings with the Pol Pot regime, and now with the Vietnamese, he discovered that only the package was different. Communism was the antithesis of freedom. Working for this corrupt government made him feel like a traitor to his people and to his conscience.

It was time to make his move.

Chapter 14
Escape!

Chanla came home the next day to an excited wife.

"Wait till you see who's here," she told him gleefully. "You won't believe it!"

As Chanla stepped into the house, a man with a neat mustache, dressed in black peasant clothes, jumped up and grasped his hands, greeting him warmly. "Bunna! Is it really you?" Chanla was excited now.

"Of course, and greetings from Division 0752 camp, from which you so cleverly deserted." Bunna spoke sternly, then began laughing. "Sit down and tell me what's happened since we parted."

As Vandy went to prepare the meal, Bunna congratulated Chanla on his high position.

"After you escaped from the secret service, we heard absolutely nothing. We were sure you had been killed."

A serious, intense young man, with a strong will, Bunna appeared tough and worldly-wise, but his emotions ran deep. He had continued with his secret service training and graduated with distinction. Subsequently he assumed command of a battalion of 1,000 rehabilitated Cambodians who had "volunteered" to fight in the New Khmer Army.

But Bunna had his own ideas about how to liberate his people, and he watched for his opportunity.

Eventually he was assigned to Krar Chae province, in the northeastern corner of Cambodia. When the time came to attack the Cambodians and secure the province for the

Vietnamese, Bunna turned his army around, and they attacked a Vietnamese unit behind them, wiping them out. His soldiers then escaped into the jungle with all the guns, ammunition, food, and loot they could carry. The group broke up into smaller units, calling themselves Freedom Fighters. Based in the jungles along the border, they grew in strength as they gradually recruited others.

But operating so near the Vietnamese, they faced great dangers and difficulties. Many were killed or captured. Bunna heard of other units forming around Phnom Penh and along the Thai-Cambodian border. Although a hefty price was put on his head, he'd decided to risk traveling to Phnom Penh. His plan was to locate these scattered groups and help organize and unite them. Bunna told Chanla that Cambodia was full of young patriots anxious to overthrow their Vietnamese oppressors.

Already disillusioned with his job, fiercely patriotic Chanla was ripe for change. He was fascinated by Bunna's plans and wanted to help him. He offered Bunna refuge in his home, and Bunna was glad to accept. Vandy worried about the risk to her husband, but she was a true oriental wife and did not oppose his desires.

Bunna located a number of resistance units in the vicinity. He would sleep during the day, then slip out at night to meet with them. Chanla began to accompany him when he could, disguising himself in peasant clothes. He listened to the various young men, so zealous and passionate, so filled with love for their homeland, so willing to make the ultimate sacrifice if necessary, and he was deeply moved. Tired of the hypocrisy and duplicity he dealt with daily, this pure idealism seemed precious indeed. He longed to join them.

One day Chanla returned home to find a stranger with Bunna.

"This is Pran," Bunna said. "He escaped a Vietnamese prison and joined a Cambodian guerrilla group operating along the Vietnamese border. He obtained a permit to travel west, and has stopped off briefly to visit Phnom Penh."

Smiling, friendly Pran was outgoing and joked a lot. He

also had a deep love for his country. Chanla and Vandy liked him right away. Now four people lived in their household.

During his months as intelligence chief, Chanla served with such straightforward dedication that the Vietnamese no longer bothered following him and checking on him. Chanla took advantage of this and helped Bunna and Pran as much as possible. He confided to his wife his increasing desire to escape the secret service and join the freedom movement. He became so obsessed with this new interest that Vandy began to fear for his safety.

One day she met Chanla at the door. The fear in her eyes made him realize something was seriously wrong.

"A young man came by today with a message from one of your friends at government headquarters," she told Chanla as soon as he got inside. "Someone has reported your involvement with the Freedom Fighters to your superiors. Your Vietnamese boss just laughed, but you know that they will start watching you."

Chanla sank into a chair. He knew he had been putting himself at considerable risk, but thought he had protected himself adequately. As director of intelligence operations, he had carefully kept the agents away from his area and from the hideouts of the Freedom Fighters. But he realized that this privilege was now over.

"Dear one," she said. "You, Bunna, and Pran must escape immediately." She looked down at her week-old infant son, and her grasp tightened on Chanla's hand. She must not let their comfort stand in the way of her husband's safety. "You must go without us," she urged. "You will have to move rapidly. Having your family along would make you too easy a target."

"You are right, dear wife." Chanla squeezed her arm and reached for his little son. "But I cannot just walk away. I need permits, papers, maps. I'll have to risk their trust in me for a little longer until I can arrange these things." He paused, trying to think.

"But Bunna and Pran must move out immediately," he continued. "They can stay with the Freedom Fighters. They are also anxious to get to the border. Perhaps I can arrange passage for the three of us."

Chanla and Vandy talked long into the night. Vandy Kim's family lived in Battambang province, not far from a popular border-crossing point. Vandy Kim had been in eastern Cambodia when the Vietnamese invaded the country, and she had been swept into the refugee camps along with her friends. She longed to return home and visit her parents, but until now it had been impossible. She helped Chanla memorize the location of her family and a brief history about them.

"Dear husband, when the agitation dies down after your escape, the rest of us will find a way to my parent's home. We will wait there for a message from you."

"Yes, yes," Chanla promised. "As soon as I reach safety I will get a message to you."

Bunna and Pran left as soon as they heard the news, giving Chanla directions as to their whereabouts. Next morning, Chanla went to work as usual, going out of his way to be friendly and cheerful with everyone. He worked with intensity and concentration. Believing he was being watched, his behavior was flawless. Outside of work, he neither met nor talked with anyone except his wife and family.

As he planned his escape, Chanla was thankful that his old friend, now Commander Oung Teur, had been called back to Vietnam the month before. It would have been especially difficult to leave this man who had trusted him and forgiven him so much. His replacement was an intelligent and efficient man who worked well with Chanla and seemed to appreciate him.

Chanla discovered that the person who had sent him the message was the mayor's wife. She was a bright, educated woman who also worked at government headquarters. She and her husband had taken a liking to Chanla early on, and they continued to keep him informed. Three days later, she told Chanla that she had intercepted an order for his arrest. It was becoming increasingly urgent that he leave.

Chanla went to his new Vietnamese superior and confided his concerns over problems in the northwestern section of the country. The intelligence groups there suffered from a lack of organization and considerable infighting. He also needed to check on border threats. Pol Pot had escaped, along with many of his followers, and was rumored to be reorganizing his army along the Thai border.

The commander was relieved to see Chanla right on top of a situation in which problems were becoming acute. He thought about the accusations he'd heard, and since nothing had been found to confirm them, he dismissed the rumors as in-house jealousies. After all, Chanla was a powerful man in the present government.

Chanla then presented his plan. "I'd like to do this job myself," he said. "Perhaps with one aide and one bodyguard. I can move faster and stir up less attention. I should be back in a week."

The project looked good, and the Vietnamese commander authorized it. His Cambodian superiors were accustomed to rubber-stamping whatever their Vietnamese "advisors" requested.

Such details had long been left for Chanla to arrange, so no one paid attention to his plans or his choice of companions. With the help of the mayor's wife, he obtained papers for Bunna and Pran. He sent word to them to meet him at the bus station the next morning. He took Vandy and the baby to Mother's house, and they had the evening meal together.

Chanla turned to his brother. "Panno, it bothers me to leave the family. I feel responsible. I had hoped we could escape together. But under the circumstances this would endanger everyone." He turned to the others. "My precious family, I entrust you to Panno's care. He is experienced in the ways of the Vietnamese, and he will find a way to get you to safety. I will pray for you and contact you as soon as I reach a safe place."

A great deal of restrained emotion was included in their farewells the next morning. Mother looked proudly at Chanla—courageous, responsible, caring deeply for his family. He was so like his father.

For Vandy, this was a most difficult time to part with her husband. She hugged her tiny infant and focused her mind on Chanla's safety. She smiled and waved, not wanting him to remember her with weeping red eyes.

No bus service existed, but a large truck left each day carrying people with travel permits. A long line waited, but Chanla and his "aides" stepped up to the officer in charge.

"Sir, I am sorry to interrupt, but I have a very important assignment in Battambang province," Chanla said respectfully. "It is urgent that I get there as soon as possible."

The officer straightened as he noted Chanla's uniform and rank. "No problem, sir. You may board immediately." He motioned toward the truck headed west. The three men cuffed each other playfully, trying not to notice the disgruntled peasants whose places they had taken.

Chanla wisely put on his oldest, most comfortable pair of boots, but otherwise was dressed in a fresh uniform. Bunna had obtained three sturdy shoulder bags, which they filled with a few necessities and a lot of rice. He and Pran wore peasant clothes to be as inconspicuous as possible. At checkpoints, soldiers and guards were so busy saluting and trying to impress Chanla, that no one searched them or looked at their papers.

When the driver reached his destination, they hopped off and began relying on their wits and training to cover the last thirty-five kilometers (twenty-two miles) to the border. With the help of a friendly taxi driver who burned Chanla's uniform and supplied peasant clothes, a kindly old farmer who hid them in an oxcart, and a lad with a couple of rabbits, they walked over the last bridge by midmorning the next day.

Feeling safe at last, they approached an open area between the bridge and the border, where they passed three Vietnamese soldiers. One of them studied the ground with a mine detector, and he suddenly looked up at Chanla.

"Look, this man is wearing Vietnamese army boots," he called to the others, speaking in Vietnamese. His companions ran toward Chanla and stood about him, inspecting the offending boots.

Chanla's heart nearly stopped. Was this to be the end? Were five years of suffering, waiting, praying, and hoping going to end here? Time seemed to stand still.

"God," he prayed. "I need another miracle. Just one more!"

Chanla and Bunna kept their faces blank and uncomprehending. They acted startled by the commotion and cast their eyes about in fear and confusion.

Pran stepped up close to the soldier who was challenging the boots and spoke in a loud, irritated voice.

"Don't you know you can buy boots like that in any market?" he said in Vietnamese. "As soon as they are scuffed a bit, the soldiers don't want them. Many Cambodian farmers wear those boots. They are heavy and durable."

Pran acted so confident and so angry that the accusing soldier backed off, intimidated. He switched to French, thinking Pran would not understand, and talked the situation over with the other two men.

"I congratulate you on your careful observation," said the first soldier, apparently the leader. "When he passed me, I did not notice the boots."

"They are probably telling the truth," the third one acknowledged. "I'm sure these things do get into peasant hands. The boys surely seem too ignorant to recognize the danger."

The soldiers administered a stern scolding and allowed them to go on. "Thank You, thank You, God," Chanla breathed, as relief flowed through his body.

As the men neared the next village, Bunna consulted his map. They found a small path leading into the forest. A few kilometers later they reached Nong Chan Camp. Bunna found several of his friends. They gladly made room for Chanla and Pran, who felt like bona fide Freedom Fighters at last.

That night, Chanla poured out his gratitude to God for the remarkable deliverance and prayed for the safety of his family. It was November 30, 1979.

When the week passed and Chanla did not return, his boss became worried. He checked with the family. They were worried too. He waited another week.

The commander finally admitted to himself that Chanla had indeed made a carefully planned escape. He became very angry. He sent out pictures of Chanla and orders to all checkpoints in the country. This man was to be arrested on sight and returned to headquarters. He wanted to deal with this traitor himself.

Trained soldiers descended on Mother's house, and each family member was interrogated separately. Vandy was located and taken to headquarters. But the family members consistently told the same story. Chanla had told them about his week's assignment, had bid them goodbye, and had taken only his army clothes. They, too, wondered why he was not back and felt worried about his safety.

Vandy cried and said she did not believe Chanla would desert her and their new son. "If he's not back, then something must have happened to him. I'm worried about him." She broke down crying again.

Hours and days of interrogations got them no further. Their story held. The soldiers did not torture them, because of Chanla's prominence. The Vietnamese took great care to appear kind and fair in the eyes of the public. Anxious to erase the hated Khmer Rouge image of cruelty and brutality, they also did not want to publicize Chanla's escape.

They decided Chanla was even more clever than they had suspected. He had not even confided his escape plans to his wife and family!

The family returned to their usual routines of buying, selling, and cultivating the gardens. Some time later, a peasant lad delivered a letter to Mother. It was from Chanla. He was safe! He urged them to come at their earliest opportunity.

Panno grew increasingly restless. He was not a patient man, and the long interrogations and constant surveillance were becoming more than he could endure. He envied Chanla and fervently wished he could have gone with him. He, too, felt drawn to the Freedom Fighters. During the past two months, he'd frequently accompanied his brother to their meetings.

But now he dared not appear to even recognize his friends on the street. It felt like prison. *Worse* than prison, Panno decided. At least in prison he was kept too busy to think.

As his isolation continued, Panno's plight became a nervous strain. He decided he needed to hurry up and figure out a way for the family to escape. They needed two things: transportation and food.

Late one evening, he traveled to a well-stocked warehouse. From the shadows, Panno watched the soldier guarding the warehouse. Panno saw a small jeep parked nearby, and wondered who it belonged to. Guards and regular soldiers were not allowed to own or drive vehicles; from experience he knew only officers and designated drivers were. He had driven these vehicles, and an idea began to form in his adventurous mind.

Some time later, a second soldier approached. "Let's go for some coffee," he called out. The guard joined him and they walked along, joking and laughing, toward a small shop two blocks away.

Now was the time! Panno rushed to the warehouse and looked inside. He saw rice, twenty-kilo (fifty-pound) bags of it, stacked one on top of the other. His eyes widened at the great quantity. People were starving only a few blocks away, and here was enough rice to feed the whole city!

Panno decided to take two bags. He would put them in the jeep. As he emerged from the warehouse with the second bag, he came face to face with the returning guard. A bright flashlight shined suddenly into his face. For a moment Panno froze.

"What are you doing?" shouted the guard. Panic and fear overwhelmed Panno, and he heaved the rice at the guard and bolted.

Panno raced for some nearby trees. Shots were fired. Panno kept running.

An hour later, Panno finally slowed down to a walk. How impulsive he had been! He rapidly walked the rest of the way home, avoiding main streets and lighted areas.

He told Mother what had happened. "They saw me. They are probably already looking for me. I must go!" Noting the alarm in Mother's eyes, he forced himself to calm down. "Mother, I kept thinking about what Chanla said. The Vietnamese care nothing for our people or our ways. Their aim is to win control of Indochina. I felt we should escape while we had the chance. I meant to help, but I got carried away." Tears filled Panno's eyes.

Mother's heart went out to her stricken son. She selected several pieces of gold for Panno to hide in his clothing. She urged him to fill his pockets with food and supplies as best he could without being obvious. She packed a small basket of food.

"Don't worry about us, dear son," Mother said, hugging him tightly. "Piteak is fifteen now and Pitura is fourteen. We'll make our way to Battambang province and stay with Vandy Kim's family until we hear from you and Chanla. You'll be able to find us there."

Mother spoke bravely, but she was crying inside. Again she was being separated from a son.

"Here is a basket of rice," she said, as she urged him to go. "If you are questioned, explain that your Great-Uncle Anth is ill, and you are taking him food. But find Chanla! Remember, he's in Nong Chan Camp."

With a mixture of fear and excitement, Panno headed west.

Chapter 15
Freedom Fighters

Bunna knew the leader of Nong Chan Camp and took Chanla and Pran to meet him the next morning.

"I'm glad to see you, old friend," the leader said. "But you've brought a very small army with you this time." They all laughed at his reference to Bunna's former battalion.

"My friends are few, but they are of the highest quality," Bunna answered. "Chanla has just left a high position in Phnom Penh's intelligence service. He knows all the important people."

Pran's experience as a guerrilla leader and recruiter was also noted, and Bunna reported on the groups of young patriots operating around Phnom Penh.

"I should also tell you that we all speak Vietnamese as well as French. Chanla does quite well in English too."

This information flashed an idea in the leader's mind. "I believe you men are just what we are looking for," he said with increasing interest. "The border area is full of so-called Freedom Fighters, but few can be trusted. Most have no education. Pol Pot and a large number of Khmer Rouge escaped to a fortress north of here, and he is trying to rebuild his army. His men constantly try to infiltrate other camps. To the west is a group called the Democratic Liberation Front. Then, of course, the New Khmer Army, with the Vietnamese, keep trying to push us deeper into the jungle."

"What about the supporters of former Prince Norodom

145

Sihanouk? What's the story there?" This was the cause closest to Bunna's heart.

"Our forces are gaining strength, but we are badly scattered. Our main job right now is to coordinate our men along the border with the freedom groups within Cambodia. Our eventual purpose, of course, is to build a united liberation force that will one day drive the Vietnamese out and bring freedom back to our country."

Freedom—Chanla must have heard that word hundreds of times during the past five years. So far, none of the concepts, in practice, had come close to the ideal he had of freedom.

But these people seemed different. The men were young, patriotic, and idealistic. No Communist harangues filled the night hours. Real freedom just might be a possibility. Chanla felt a surge of hope and excitement.

The leader was talking again. "We need some trusted couriers to coordinate our groups with the freedom units within Cambodia. We need them to carry messages, reports, instructions, and permits between their leaders and ours. They will arrange payments, including transfers of gold and of arms."

The men listened with growing interest as the leader continued. "We need responsible men we can trust. These men should look and behave like common peasants, yet should be skilled enough to elude border patrols, avoid traps, and recognize friend from foe. You speak the needed languages, you've learned survival skills, and you are wise enough to arrange beneficial deals. I think we have found our couriers!"

Chanla, especially, was delighted over this turn of events. Though he hated the enemy, he still had trouble squaring his conscience with the duties of a soldier. He could not imagine himself killing anyone. He breathed a prayer of thanks.

"What kind of uniforms are we to wear? What identification will we carry?" Pran, as usual, was the one to voice their questions. "Will we be armed?"

"Keep the clothes you are wearing. We want you to blend in with the peasants. You will be given appropriate passwords, permits, and other papers as you need them. To defend yourselves, you will carry small guns that can easily be hidden."

When Red Cross representatives appeared later that day, their usefulness became immediately apparent. French was the only common language, and Chanla was able to arrange a sizeable shipment of supplies for the camp.

Chanla and his friends began exploring the territory between their camp and the official borders. They befriended fellow Freedom Fighters as well as the peasants in nearby villages. Their honest, straightforward dealings and lack of manipulation quickly gained the respect and trust of the others. Their freedom of movement and their valued status with the leaders rapidly became the envy of the camp.

Things were going well. Chanla felt an increasing optimism for the future. Perhaps he wouldn't have to leave his country after all! The different groups camped along the border all considered themselves Khmer Serei (free Khmer) and called themselves Freedom Fighters. If they could agree on common aims and philosophies, and rally under a capable leader, they would indeed become a force to be reckoned with.

Though inspired by his new opportunities, Chanla missed his wife and son. He wondered if the Vietnamese had sought to punish the family. Would Panno be able to bring them to Battambang? He began building a little house outside of camp, a short way into the jungle. They would be relatively safe there. The men at Nong Chan Camp were respectful of families, and the men in nearby camps did not bother the powerful fort.

One day Panno appeared. The brothers greeted each other exuberantly, but Panno read the question in Chanla's face. "Mother urged me to go on ahead," he explained. "They were watching us day and night. She feared they would find some pretext to arrest me, for vengeance."

"But who will bring the family?" Chanla was alarmed now.

"Mother is very ingenious," Panno assured him. "She

planned to start for Vandy's home in a few days."

Panno had reached another camp, Nong Samith, referred to as "007." He had been welcomed and had found several friends there. In fact, one of their distant cousins was a camp leader.

"For the first time since I can remember, I'm excited about my work. I feel I'm doing something positive for my country."

Panno returned to his camp, leaving Chanla with fresh concerns. He sent a letter to Vandy Kim's home in nearby Battambang province. He prayed several times a day for the safety of his family.

Left on her own, Mother lost no time. She took Piteak into her confidence. Serious-minded and dependable, he was becoming more and more like his father.

Some of the village people avoided Mother and gossiped cruelly about her "traitor sons," saying the curse of the gods was on the family. Others grew jealous of her business acumen and relative prosperity. But a few were sympathetic and helpful. They brought news regarding the political situation, and they gave her advice about travel.

The family continued to put on a consistent front. They fretted about Chanla and Panno. Why hadn't the boys returned? What had happened to them?

Often Mother wept while talking about them, telling friends that they, too, might have been killed, like Father. She visited Chanla's old headquarters, urging them to continue searching for her son.

These details were not lost on the guards who continued to watch them. The family was obviously devastated, with only helpless women and children left. In time the soldiers lost interest.

One day Mother and Vandy Kim went to the head of their village and explained the problem: their menfolk were gone, they were unable to support the large family, and they needed to find relatives to help them. They asked for permits to travel to Vandy Kim's home village in Battambang province. To their surprise, the permits were readily granted.

The next problem was finding transportation. It would take about four weeks on foot. They'd done that before, but with no menfolk, no vehicles, and a new baby, Mother doubted they could do it again.

Mother looked at Grandma, nearing her eightieth birthday. She went about her chores with energy and cheerfulness. When Grandpa died, Mother had invited Grandma into her home, planning to care for her for life. But during the past five years, their roles had reversed. While Mother worked in the fields or shuttled back and forth to the city, Grandma had cared for the home, for her daughter, and for the children.

"Mother, I do believe you are stronger than you were ten years ago. You work as hard as I do, and you never complain."

"You can blame that on the Khmer Rouge," said Grandma, smiling at the irony. "But I do feel well. I'm healthier now than I thought possible for a woman of my age."

Piteak had been investigating, and he told Mother that with their permits they would be able to travel by train. A solution! Friends helped them carry their things to the railroad station.

Trains came frequently, but each was filled to capacity. They waited; one day, two days, three. They camped beside the railroad track and took turns keeping watch. Though small for his age, Piteak had a man-sized sense of responsibility. He hardly slept. He looked after details, watched the children, kept things organized. Prok, now fourteen, stayed right by his side.

"Daughter, I believe you have two more sons growing into their father's shoes," Grandmother said, pride in her voice.

"Of course. I never doubted it." Mother pinched Prok and winked at Piteak.

After seven days and nights of waiting, they were able to board a train. The crowding and heat inside the railroad cars nearly smothered them, but they eventually reached their destination. From the station, they piled into a motorcycle taxi, which took them to Vandy Kim's home.

Vandy knelt respectfully before her mother for a few moments, and then they clasped each other. It had been nearly ten years since they'd seen each other.

"Look at your little grandson," Vandy said with glistening eyes. "His name is Bunarith. It means 'strength,' 'power to live.' That's what he symbolizes to me." She hugged the two-month-old baby and laid him in his grandmother's arms. "He looks just like his father," she added.

Chanla, Bunna, and Pran built themselves a shack inside Nong Chan Camp. They relished their privacy, and they frequently entertained friends. Chanla openly studied his piece of Bible.

Except for the absence of his family, Chanla felt more at peace than he'd been for a long time. No longer was he a slave for a mindless Angka. No longer did he feel coerced into serving a government he believed to be working against the best interests of his people. He was helping lay the foundations for the future freedom of his country!

He worked diligently, developing a loyal network of contacts among Cambodian patriots, transferring food, money, and ammunition to them for their people within Cambodia. He was honest, dependable, fair. He didn't take advantage of them. In return, they gave him their respect and friendship.

Although the three men constantly faced opportunities to personally profit from their transactions, they were too patriotic to consider such temptations. Their leader continued to give them his full trust, despite having no way of adequately checking on them.

About three months after Chanla arrived, a rough and violent group of men attacked their camp. The Nong Chan leader immediately raised a white truce flag and met with the rebel chief.

"What do you want?" he asked in a conciliatory tone. "We are Cambodian brothers. It is wrong for us to fight and kill each other. What purpose does it serve?"

The rebels would settle for nothing less than occupation and control of the fort.

"Give us about four hours. My men will withdraw

peaceably, and the fort will be yours."

Incredibly, that is what they did. The Nong Chan group set up temporary headquarters a few kilometers away in the jungle, and the ruffians took over the fort. Chanla and his friends fled with them, but after a few days they risked a trip to meet their clients at the Cambodian border. It was without incident. On the next trip they were accosted by the new fort occupants.

"Look at us," Chanla said, stretching out his arms with open hands. "We are not soldiers. We are peasants."

"Search us if you like," Pran chimed in, hoping they wouldn't. "We are only securing supplies for our village."

This seemed to satisfy the patrol for the moment, but the men felt uneasy.

In about two weeks, reinforcements arrived, and the rebels were driven out. Messages sent to the people in the jungle stated that it was safe to return, and most of them did. Their original leaders, however, were not reinstated, and rumors circulated that they had been executed.

The new bosses of Nong Chan Camp lost no time in contacting Chanla, Bunna, and Pran, asking them to continue their work. A slight adjustment would be made, however. Would they take on two assistants, a young man named Harn and a young woman named Mo Del?

Mo Del and Harn were bright and likeable; the five got along well. They lived and worked together, sharing everything. Outwardly, things appeared to be going well, although the three friends felt considerably less secure with the new leadership.

Chanla also became increasingly concerned over the infighting and corruption growing within the camp. The soldiers seemed to be spending more time and energy fighting each other than the enemy. Each "leader" endeavored to enlarge his power over the other leaders. Each camp isolated itself more and more from sister camps. Each began making its own rules. Selfishness and greed spread like a virus, and Chanla felt an ache growing inside him.

Pitura saw it first. "Mama," she shouted, "here it is— Chanla's letter!" The family gathered, and she read aloud:

Dear Family:

I am well, and am preparing a small house for you. Enclosed is a map showing the exact location of my camp, the Nong Chan Camp. It is large and well known. Find an experienced guide to bring you here. I will look for you soon. Be careful. I'm praying for your safety. Panno is in a camp nearby.

Chanla

Mother knew the border region was a dangerous place. The retreating Khmer Rouge had planted many land mines and booby traps to discourage the Vietnamese from following them. No roads and few landmarks existed. The various groups camped along the border continually fought over territorial rights. Roving bands of bandits were also a menace.

But none of this mattered to the Dok family right now. Mother went immediately to headquarters to obtain a permit for travel to the border village. Vandy felt torn over leaving her family so soon.

"Go, my daughter," her mother urged. "You must join your husband. Since my husband's death, I have no interest in staying under this oppressive regime either. I have copied the map. We will join you soon."

The family traveled to the border village, and Mother went in search of a guide. She sent up a special prayer for help to Chanla's God because she knew that many who posed as guides were merely robbers in disguise. They would lead unsuspecting families a few kilometers into the jungle, rob them of their possessions, and then desert them.

"I've found a guide," Mother told them when she returned. "I inquired everywhere, and this one has the best reputation." She stopped, fighting a rush of emotion. "He demanded a high price, and there is no guarantee." She hesitated again, controlling herself, not wanting the family to sense her fear. "But we must take the risk. Chanla and Panno are waiting for us."

Mother found an oxcart and bargained hard with the driver, who reluctantly agreed to accompany them. Grandmother and the two small girls rode on top of their bundles, and the others walked. Vandy placed her baby in a sling at her side.

After they left the village and went into the jungle, they stopped to regroup. Piteak, the worrier, positioned himself behind the guide to head off possible trouble. Then came Mother and Pitura. The oxcart and brother Prok brought up the rear.

The guide knew his business. He avoided checkpoints and guarded outposts. He seemed to have exceptionally sensitive ears. Several times he quickly pulled the group together, and a few minutes later men would pass.

"Robbers," he muttered. They understood. The bandits would hesitate to attack a group, while they would not worry about attacking a straggler or two.

The man told Piteak that he made the trip once or twice a week, sometimes guiding people, at other times picking up or delivering supplies. Piteak suspected he was a smuggler.

As the night wore on, the family breathed easier. Though they were weary, their increasing anticipation fueled their energies. Their guide seemed to be keeping his bargain. Near daylight, however, he stopped and demanded more money.

"We are nearly there, and you are all safe. I have taken a great risk for you," he said.

"We appreciate what you have done, but I have already paid you a high price," Mother reminded him. But she handed him another gold coin.

Satisfied, he walked on for about half a kilometer.

"This is as far as I go," he announced. He pointed ahead. "Nong Chan Camp is about five kilometers (three miles) in that direction. The men guard their turf fiercely, but will not harm a group of women and children." With that, he was gone.

Somewhat uncertain, the group pressed on. When they arrived at the camp, the sun was already rising in the sky. A soldier disappeared inside to call Chanla.

Expecting a handsome, clean-cut young soldier, the family was surprised to see a long-haired man in peasant clothes running toward them. In a moment, Chanla was hugging his young wife and reaching for his son.

"Is this my little Rith?" Chanla exclaimed, tears of joy spilling down his cheeks. "He is about three times bigger than I remember."

"He was only a week old," Vandy reminded him, her own face wet. "He's three months now."

Chanla handed the baby back and knelt before his mother.

"Mother, you are better than two men," he exclaimed. "How did you accomplish such a miracle?"

"We couldn't have done it without your wife," Mother said, respect in her voice. "Vandy Kim is an unselfish and courageous young woman. We received permits to go to her home, and she and her family sheltered and protected us. She carries her share of the burdens and more, and she does not complain."

Chanla took a fresh look at his wife. How proud he was of her!

"Come, I've prepared a place for you in the jungle," Chanla said as he led them to the little house. The children whooped with joy and went off to explore their new surroundings, while Mother and Grandma admired Chanla's work. They began unloading the cart.

Vandy, however, was in another world. In her husband's arms once more, the strain and worry of the past weeks dissolved. She kissed him again and again, wept on his chest, and held him close. The others discreetly withdrew as the young lovers vented their pent-up feelings, their loneliness melting into the joy of reunion.

With the house completed, gardens were planted, and life settled into a peacefulness they'd not known for the past five years. Chanla brought food and other necessities from camp, and he spent many nights with them as well. Panno sent a message telling of his joy at being reunited with many relatives and old friends. He would visit soon.

How long would this hiatus of peace, this little slice of paradise, last? Chanla spoke encouragingly of the Freedom Fighters. Support within Cambodia was growing. One day, they hoped to be strong enough to strike.

Despite the positive talk, Mother's practiced eyes noted that Chanla was becoming increasingly troubled.

Chapter 16
Ultimate Double Cross

Chanla stared in shocked disbelief. "What do you mean, you are spies?"

Bunna was stunned into silence. Pran jumped up, eyes flashing, feelings roiling into a torrent of words: "We've worked together for two months. We've trusted you with everything we know. We've treated you like family. And—and—now you plan to have us shot!"

"Hush, hush," begged Mo Del, with fear in her own eyes. "No one must hear us. That's why we're telling you. We aren't spies anymore. We want to join you."

Harn broke in. "Our new leaders were suspicious of you. You had too much freedom. They believed you were plotting to form your own group, your own command."

"So they asked us to work with you, to spy on you, and to report every suspicious or unusual activity." Mo Del's voice trembled. "They especially wanted us to keep track of your financial transactions."

Harn took over. "We did this for several weeks. But we could find absolutely nothing even questionable."

"You are the most honest, conscientious, patriotic young men we have ever met! We've learned to respect you, to *care* for you. We want to be on your side."

"We'll send token reports to our leaders, as we've been doing, so we don't arouse suspicion. But our loyalties are to you." Harn spoke passionately, open hands reaching toward them.

155

Emotions were raw. They were putting their lives on the line. Chanla, Bunna, and Pran calmed down. They began talking about what to do.

"I've been worried about the conditions of our camp," admitted Chanla. "The Freedom Fighters are behaving like robbers, pirates. They aren't protecting the peasants as before, and nobody seems to care."

"The leaders of each group are jealous and suspicious of each other," added Bunna. "There's infighting within our own camp. I'm sure the present leadership eliminated the former leaders, who were my friends."

"That's classified information, but it's true," said Mo Del. "We're totally disgusted with them. They're more interested in their own status, their own profits, than they are in the fate of Cambodia."

The five friends talked long into the night, planning their future and discussing activities and projects that might yet improve the declining situation.

"These men need to be reminded of what we endured under the Khmer Rouge, and of the true intentions of our Vietnamese 'liberators.' " said Pran. "We need to get back to basics, like unity and cooperation."

But nobody felt very optimistic. A chill enveloped Chanla's heart as he realized they were working under suspicion. Their days could well be numbered. They must be very careful. Chanla decided to delay telling his family. He mustn't worry them unnecessarily.

During the next few days, business continued as usual. Perhaps, they thought, they had exaggerated the problems in their minds. Then, like a ripened boil, everything came to a head.

A fellow soldier, jealous of Harn and Mo Del's growing influence, reported suspected treachery. At 9:00 a.m., two motorcycles arrived at the shack to carry them across the compound to the command post. The guards loaded Bunna and Pran on one motorcycle, and Mo Del and Harn on the other. They told Chanla to wait, they'd be back for him.

Chanla felt apprehensive, but he did as he was told. Besides, why should he be worried? There had been no hint of trouble. Meetings like this were not exactly un-usual. It was probably another routine briefing.

Chanla waited for two hours, but no one came for him. Feeling hungry, he went in search of something to eat. Apparently it wasn't important that he be at the meeting. However, he began to wonder why the others didn't return.

In the early afternoon, he walked to his home in the jungle. He tried to shake off his uneasiness, but he sensed something was wrong. Was God somehow protecting him, getting him away from the others? He sat in front of his hut where he could watch the road. Hearing a motorcycle approaching, he was startled to see Harn. Chanla rose to call him, but saw a second cycle following close behind. Apparently an armed soldier was escorting him back to the fort. A few moments later, shots erupted.

After escaping the Vietnamese secret service in Phnom Penh, Chanla had let his hair grow full and long as a protection against being recognized. It had become his trademark. Now he asked Mother to crop his hair very short. He confided the situation to her. He changed his clothes, and Mother helped him pack his papers and valu-ables into his special pockets.

He went to find Vandy, who burst out laughing at the sight of his short, spiky hair. But the look on Chanla's face sobered her quickly.

"If I have to flee, I'll contact Panno. He's at Camp 007, about ten kilometers (6.2 miles) from here." Chanla spoke in a matter-of-fact tone. Vandy said nothing, but sat close to him on the step.

Later, a boy about ten years old appeared, asking for Chanla. No one remembered seeing the boy before. He handed Chanla a note and left without a word. It had been hastily scribbled on a small scrap of paper in a strange ink. He didn't recognize the handwriting. The message was brief:

You must escape quickly. Your friends have been killed.

"Dear God in heaven," Chanla prayed in panic, "what shall I do now?"

Just then, he heard approaching voices. He darted behind the house and was sprinting toward the jungle when
Mother called to him.

"It's all right, Chanla. They are friends." Turning
around, he recognized the young men. They were Freedom
Fighters from the interior of Cambodia with whom he dealt
on a regular basis. During the past five months, close
friendships had developed, and these men frequently
dropped by Chanla's jungle house, sometimes staying
overnight.

Chanla's emotions were in turmoil. He was glad to see
friends, but realized they were in danger also. He explained to them what had happened, and about the note
he'd received a few moments earlier.

"We'll go with you. We'll escape together," they told him
after a brief consultation. "We can't risk going to the fort,
and it would be dangerous to return to Cambodia under
the present uncertainties."

Chanla felt relieved. He admired these courageous, loyal
young men. They, too, were constantly risking their lives
for their country.

"Let's head for Nong Samith Camp 007. My brother is
there, and my cousin is one of the leaders."

Chanla bade his family goodbye. Rith, now five months
old, gurgled happily as his father hugged him. Vandy
anointed him with kisses. "We'll see you soon," she said,
unable to restrain a smile at how funny he looked. Again,
she would not cry.

"Mother, keep everyone together and wait until you hear
from us. Panno and I will send for you as soon as we can."
Grandmother pressed rice cakes into their hands. They
had no time for supper.

It was nearing dusk as they entered the jungle. The six
men traveled rapidly, trying to get as far as possible before
darkness hampered them.

A few minutes later, one of the men suddenly stopped
and motioned to the others. Chanla stiffened in horror.
The mutilated body of his friend Bunna lay before Chanla,
its decapitated head upside down a few feet away.

Something broke inside Chanla. He was beyond tears,

but he couldn't stop his thoughts. His life seemed to reel forward and backward through the insufferable horror of the past few years. War was senseless, no matter who played the game. One side was no better than the other when both resorted to the same brutal tactics.

Sickened with grief and revulsion, Chanla stumbled on. In a few minutes they passed Mo Del's body, also decapitated, and with breasts cut off as well. So this was the fate of courageous young Cambodian patriots in so-called Freedom Camps. Horrified and heartsick, he felt drained of further hope for the deliverance of his country. He'd had enough. He was determined to escape this insanity, this endless merry-go-round of death.

As they walked in the darkness, they heard voices and saw darting beams from flashlights. Men noisily tramped about, searching the area. The fleeing group immediately dropped to the ground, pretending to be asleep. Chanla pulled a scarf over his face, according to Cambodian custom. He didn't move a muscle, but his heart pounded so loudly he was afraid it could be heard. He sent an urgent prayer heavenward.

Shortly, they were discovered. "Get up!" the leader commanded, as he kicked the first man he reached. He inspected him carefully with his flashlight, then continued through the group. He wouldn't trust this job to anyone else.

"Don't bother with these guys," he yelled as he finished examining the fourth man. "We only want Chanla, the one with the long hair."

Chanla was next. Despite his short hair, Chanla knew that if this man glimpsed his face, he would be recognized.

Chanla roused slowly, as from a deep sleep. He got up as deliberately as possible, yawning and turning slightly to one side. He stretched, bringing his right arm up along the side of his face and across his forehead. Keeping his eyes averted, and with a slight turn of his head, he made sure only his profile was visible. The leader was getting impatient. He switched his flashlight to the sixth man, who sat up and faced him.

"He isn't here," the leader announced, and the twelve-man patrol passed on. "He should be easy to find, with that bushy hair . . . ." The voices receded in the distance.

Chanla sank back to the ground, emotionally spent. He now knew how Daniel must have felt when he'd faced the lions in the lion's den.

"We must keep going," his friends urged after a reasonable time. "In daylight you will be recognized by anyone from Nong Chan." Taking their bearings from the stars, they continued through the forest.

By early morning, Nong Samith Camp 007 loomed ahead. They found Panno and told him everything. "This camp is under a different leadership. You will be safe here," Panno told them. "However, I advise you to stay in the jungle for a few days, in case any spies or search parties come through."

After helping them locate a hiding place in the jungle, Panno went back to camp and returned in about an hour with food and drink. He motioned to Chanla, and they walked a short way together.

"Brother," Panno's tone was serious. "I've gotten permission to go to Nong Chan Camp to get the family." He stopped and looked at Chanla. "They are in great danger."

Chapter 17
Panno Comes Through

After Chanla left, Mother anxiously paced about, wondering what to do. She knew her son was once again a hunted man, and she prayed to God for his safety. She slept little. At breakfast she looked so tired and distracted that Piteak grew concerned.

"Mother, let's pack our things," he suggested. "We may have to leave in a hurry." As if to punctuate their concerns, gunfire broke out again in the fort, continuing intermittently the rest of the morning.

As they gathered their things and tied them into bundles, they were startled by heavy footsteps on the front porch and a booming voice.

"Well, Mother, are you ready to go?"

Mother whirled around, embracing Panno joyfully. She tousled his hair and patted his bulging muscles. She had not seen him since they parted in Phnom Penh, four months earlier.

Panno saw the worry in her eyes. "Chanla is safe," he said. "We've hidden him in the forest." Then he looked directly at Mother, and his tone changed. "But *you* are in great danger. Soldiers could come at any moment. Let's leave quickly."

Sometime earlier, Mother had traded a few of their remaining possessions for an old bicycle. It came in handy now. As they loaded it, Panno continued to urge haste.

"Take as little as possible so we can move rapidly. All of

161

our lives will depend on it."

They carried a few more things by hand, but much was left behind. Piteak and Prok pushed the bicycle, and Mother and Pitura helped Vandy with the baby. Panno was their guide and bodyguard.

Grandma eyed his large rifle. "Are you sure you know how to shoot that thing?" Pitura tittered, Prok laughed out loud, and the others began to smile. The tension broke. Mother teased him about his strange uniform. The children took turns running up to him, touching the rifle, and giggling.

As they walked, Mother studied her second son. Improved food rations had erased the skeletal look. His hair had grown longer. Panno's energy and enthusiasm were undimmed, but his impulsiveness had been tempered. At twenty-two, he was more mature, more sure of himself.

Mother finally spoke. "Son, what is your camp like? Are you happy there?"

Panno chose his words carefully. "I have been treated well. A cousin of ours is one of the camp leaders, and many of the soldiers are my friends from the past. Conditions are much better than in the labor camps."

Panno sighed, looking a little sad. "I'm troubled about the future," he confessed. "The Freedom Fighters along the border have splintered into several factions, and at times they attack one another. The Vietnamese constantly search for us. Even within our own camp there are power struggles. Few of us are satisfied with our progress."

Mother realized that Panno's experiences were paralleling Chanla's in many ways. Both were becoming disillusioned about the resistance movement.

Panno changed the subject. He was expressing himself too openly.

"For Chanla's safety, we have temporarily hidden him. The men at Nong Chan probably suspect he will come to my camp. We don't want to take any chances."

He turned to Mother. "But the rest of you don't have to worry. The soldiers respect peasants. We can build another little hut nearby, and I can bring rice from camp."

"What about Thailand? Aren't we close to the border?

Can't we just walk on over there?"

Panno had to smile at his mother's solution. She could be optimistic, even in the worst of times.

"Well, maybe," Panno mused. "There is a large Thai refugee camp about thirteen kilometers north of us. But many dangers lie between here and there. Mines are hidden on the roads and in the forests. Although the Pol Pot people claim they had to do this to keep the Thai people from attacking, it's more likely that it was intended to discourage the rest of us from leaving Cambodia. Those mines took a terrible toll at first, killing or wounding about eighty percent of the early groups that went over."

"Don't soldiers patrol the borders?" Piteak asked. "Isn't anyone in charge?"

"Neither country takes responsibility for this piece of no-man's land. Robbers abound, pouncing like tigers on defenseless refugees. They don't hesitate to strip their victims and carry out humiliating body searches."

Panno looked at his sixteen-year-old sister, with her beautiful dark hair cascading over her shoulders, reaching nearly to her waist. Pitura's hair was her most distinctive feature, and she was proud of it. She had been nurturing it since village days. Her drab clothes and gray surroundings became more bearable when she combed her hair and dreamed of being a beautiful movie star. She would pretend her crude peasant clothes were of silky satin. When she was alone, she practiced graceful little dances.

As Pitura matured, she attracted increasing notice and felt flattered by the admiring glances that came her way. Mother worried about this, but couldn't deny her daughter her only bit of vanity. Mother was extremely protective, however, and Pitura was not allowed out of the house unless in the company of her mother and brothers.

But Panno decided the time had come for his sister to face present realities.

"Young women are especially desirable targets for border thieves and ruffians. They have no behavior code, as we do. After stripping and robbing their victims, these men often take turns raping them. If a girl resists, she could be killed. Particularly desirable girls are kidnapped and carried into the jungle."

"No! No! I don't want to escape to Thailand!" Pitura cried out, eyes large with fear and terror. "We can stay here and live as we have."

Panno's tone changed. "Don't worry, dear sister. We'll plan carefully. I'll assemble several families together in a group and find a guide who speaks the Thai language and understands their military patrol system. But it will take time."

At the next stop, Pitura braided her hair and coiled it into a bun on her head. She wound a piece of cloth around it. Vandy also covered her head and part of her face with her scarf.

By early evening, the family reached Chanla. Exhaustion had finally taken its toll, and the six men were sound asleep. Panno had told Mother of Chanla's harrowing escape. Her eyes stung with tears of relief. Surely God's protective hand was over this remarkable son of hers.

In the morning, Pitura soberly asked Mother to cut her hair. Mother did so in silence, feeling deep compassion for the struggle within.

The men fashioned a crude shelter with their bare hands. No one had an ax or even a knife large enough to cut tree branches. They searched the jungle for pieces of wood, vines, and bits of thatch. Their primitive, limited hut would protect them from the sun but was of little use during rainstorms. They were thankful to be safe, however, and to be together. At night they unrolled their mats on the bare ground and slept without mosquito nets, which had been left behind.

They became aware of others in the jungle around them. Some were the families of men in the fort, and others were refugees waiting to cross over into Thailand. Many more were displaced people who had moved near the fort for safety. A few had built fairly substantial houses and even dug wells.

Chanla's friends were becoming restless. It was soon

evident that no one from Nong Chan would risk coming to Camp 007, even for Chanla. The men talked over their alternatives, and two of them decided to return to Cambodia. Chanla gave them the gold, valuables, and papers he had with him pertaining to his former job. The other three chose to join Panno and the Freedom Fighters in Camp 007.

The next few weeks were especially difficult. Panno brought what rice he could from camp, but some days he was unable to come at all. Without their mosquito nets, the family began suffering bouts of malaria. Their water supply became polluted, and dysentery and other illnesses appeared. Panno tried to get medicine, but the scarce supply was reserved for the soldiers in the fort. A violent storm blew away a precious sheet of corrugated tin that Panno had found. Panno and Chanla then slept on the roof, using their bodies to help protect their loved ones.

Waiting her turn at the well, one day Vandy spotted her mother! Both were surprised and overjoyed.

"Dear Mother, you did make it after all!" Vandy's voice was full of joy.

"Yes, Vandy, several of us are here, including my sister. Come and see where we are staying."

"Mother mine, at last we'll get to know each other," an exuberant Vandy exclaimed. "And you can enjoy your grandson." The relationship became a bright spot in an otherwise trying period.

Chanla was wrestling with his own problems. Even as he fled Nong Chan, he realized that his gun, knife, and Bible were back in the shack inside the fort. He felt defenseless and vulnerable without them. A knife was also a survival tool, used to cut one's way through the forest, to build shelters and hiding places, to kill and cut up wild game, and to make kindling.

But he missed his Bible most of all. It had been preserved for five years, through all kinds of hazards. He had taken it into Nong Chan Camp because he had more time to study it there.

Time dragged. Chanla wandered about, restless and troubled. He had no heart to join the Freedom Fighters at

Panno's camp and avoided even entering the fort. He was sick of hypocrisy, senseless killings, and useless wars. He remembered his dream of long ago, about the helicopters carrying the family to freedom. He became increasingly obsessed with a desire to escape from Cambodia and find a new life.

Grandma once more presided over the meals and watched the children. Vandy frequently visited her mother. Piteak, Pitura, and Mother circulated among the families camped around the fort and discovered several old friends and even some distant relatives.

Mother learned that a small border village lay about five kilometers (three miles) away. Though risks were involved, Mother announced she was going there the next day. If several went together, robbers would have less chance of attacking. Chanla and Piteak agreed to accompany her. Pitura wanted to help but felt fearful after Panno's stories. Vandy put her arms around her husband.

"Dear one, I will go too. If anything happens, let it happen to both of us."

Chanla's eyes softened. His precious Vandy. What an unusual girl! Her unselfish love tempered and strengthened him.

They started for the village, pushing the bicycle. Chanla's training helped them elude outposts and checkpoints and spot booby traps and other dangers. Several men whom they feared might be robbers walked by, but they did not stop.

The village had small markets with clothing and other wares not seen for many years in Cambodia. They knew these items must have been smuggled from Thailand. Mother exchanged some of her gold and bought cloth, needles, thread, and a few luxury items like watches and cigarette lighters. She was a born businesswoman, outbargaining the most hard-nosed salesman. She later traded these items to the Freedom Fighters and others for food and missing necessities like mosquito nets.

Still, a large void remained in Chanla's life. He prayed several times a day. He told the children Bible stories about Abraham, Moses, and David, reminding them again that God could use very bad circumstances and still bring good things out of them. Vandy was often at her mother's, but the others sat nearby. The concept was strange to them. The gods they'd known cared little for the individual. It was up to each one of them to improve himself, do good deeds, and thus earn his way up the ladder, hopefully achieving a higher or better life in the next reincarnation.

During the night hours, Chanla felt especially close to his Lord.

"Thank You, dear God, for Your incredible providences in preserving our lives. Few have survived and remained together as we have. I know You must have some very special plans for us."

Chanla began repeating every Bible promise he could remember, though he wasn't absolutely sure of the wording.

> "*I will never leave you nor forsake you.*"
> "*I am with you and will keep you wherever you go.*"
> "*The angel of the Lord camps around those who fear Him and delivers them.*"

Chanla had certainly proved these promises in his own experience.

> "*Cast all your care upon Him, for He cares for you.*"
> "*Lo I am with you always, even unto the end.*"

"Yes, Lord, I believe Your Word, and I love and trust You. Help me not to feel discouraged. Lead our family to peace and freedom if that is Your will."

Calmed at last, Chanla slept.

In his spare time, Panno was busy arranging passage for his family. He located a guide he trusted and rounded up about twenty-five other families waiting to cross the border.

Panno appeared at the hut early one afternoon.

"Everything is arranged," he announced. "Mother went with me, and we hired the guide. My friends are ready to escort us. We'll leave at sundown."

During their two-month stay near Camp 007, Grandma suffered from malaria and exposure. Mother knew she was too weak to make the trip on foot, so she purchased a hammock and pole and hired two young men to carry her.

Vandy sought out Chanla. "Sweet one, I've been talking to my mother, and she refuses to leave without her sister. Please understand. We have been so recently reunited that I cannot bear to part with her yet. I might never see her again. Let me stay a while longer. I'm sure I can persuade her to come with the next group."

"No, Vandy, my dear one, no! I can't risk another separation from you and our son. There are too many dangers."

But Vandy Kim could be stubborn. She had made up her mind.

"Then I will stay with you," Chanla said heatedly. "I can't leave you here alone with the baby."

"But, Chanla, it's *your* life that is in danger, not mine. You must go. Your whole family depends on you. You are the father now. I know how to survive, you know that. I'll be careful."

Chanla was reluctant, but she continued to urge him. Finally he gave her all the rest of his gold and valuables. He held her in his arms and prayed for God's protection.

As she kissed him again and again, she tried to reassure him. "Dear husband, my mother, Rith, and I will meet you before another moon is full. That is a promise."

About two hours after dark, the group followed their guide toward Khao I Dang Refugee Camp in Thailand. Panno's six armed friends ringed the group, prominently displaying their Chinese-made AK-47 assault rifles. Pitura carefully stayed in the middle of the group with a heavy hood over her head.

About an hour later they encountered a group of Khmer Serei (Freedom Fighters) who ordered them to stop. Panno stepped forward, and they recognized him. Panno's outgoing, gregarious nature had made him many friends in the region.

"OK, Panno. If this is your group, you may go."

The little band passed on quietly. About midnight, they heard voices and saw flashlights. Panno suspected robbers. However, at the sight of the armed escort, the men vanished. They weren't prepared for a shootout.

Near the edge of the forest the guide ordered everyone to lie down. He then walked on alone toward the Thai military policeman guarding the passage to the refugee camp. They bargained a while in Thai. When the guide returned, he told them that each person must pay 100 baht (about $4.00) to pass this point. He collected the money from the refugees and delivered it to the guard. They were then instructed to lie quietly until the M.P. gave the signal. Then they must cross quickly.

Chanla crawled over to Panno and asked what it all meant.

"It's bribe money," Panno whispered. "If this guard can get us through without another guard seeing us, he gets to keep all the money. Otherwise we'll have to pay more."

Chanla had to smile at the irony. Thailand might be free of oppression and fear, but in some quarters, at least, greed was alive and well.

The signal came, and the refugees ran through the checkpoint. Their escorts bade them goodbye and returned to the fort. The guide took them to the entrance of Khao I Dang Camp.

Freedom! Safety! Chanla felt like they had entered the Promised Land. The Thais were friendly and helpful. The refugees were given food, clothes, and small houses. Hospital care and medicines were available to everyone. The newcomers received anti-malarial pills and were treated for lice. They got baths. Clean clothes. Comfortable cots with mosquito nets. *And no more pig's food!* They received *good* rice for every meal, which they were allowed to prepare themselves.

The camp had schools, and during the next few days, the younger ones enrolled. Chanla and Panno signed up for English classes. Mother, Grandma, Panno, and Chanla explored the camp, looking for someone they knew. Despite the thousands of refugees, they were able to locate an occasional relative and a few friends. Panno joined several sports activities, excelling in many of them.

One afternoon, Chanla noticed a man approaching who seemed extremely familiar.

"*Pran! Am I seeing a ghost?*"

Pran was equally astonished. "Chanla—I thought you were dead!"

Chanla could scarcely contain his feelings. "Come, let's find a quiet place to talk."

Pran told him what had happened that day. Arriving at headquarters, the four of them found their leaders hostile and angry.

"Take that motorcycle and bring Chanla," the leader barked at Harn.

As Harn left, the guards tied the rest of them up. When they got to Pran, they had run out of rope. The guards found some pieces of string and finally had him secured to their satisfaction.

During the interrogation that followed, the commander became concerned that Harn did not return. He sent one of the guards on the other motorcycle to find him. Their captors were tense and nervous, frequently looking out of the windows.

Their interrogation was harsh. The three were accused of being traitors, of stealing gold and causing insurrection in the camp. Deciding to separate them, their captors took Mo Del to another room, and then went outside to place Bunna onto a truck. Pran slipped his bonds and vanished out the back door. He made his way into the forest and found shelter with a peasant family. Later he heard that Harn was found, escorted back to the fort, and shot.

"I suspected as much," Chanla told him. "I was waiting in my jungle house and saw Harn and another man drive into camp about midafternoon. I feared the worst when I heard the shots." He told Pran about his own escape and about seeing the bodies of Bunna and Mo Del. "I thought sure you had been murdered also." The memories were keen, and Chanla's heart ached once more for his friends.

"I tried to send you a note," said Pran, "but I didn't know whether you received it. I wrote it with the juice of a root and gave it to a village lad. Word reached us a few days later that a serious uprising had taken place in camp and many had been killed. That's the last I'd heard of Bunna, Mo Del, or you."

"I grieve deeply for our friends," Chanla said, reflecting. After a moment he stood, smiled, and put his hand on his friend's shoulder. "But I'm glad to see you alive. It cheers my heart. We both have a chance for a new life."

A new life! Chanla relished every detail. Eating until his stomach was full, wearing what he pleased, sleeping a night through without fear—he had almost forgotten what it was like! Mother and Grandma laughed and joked once more. The children played noisily, and people began to speak openly without fear.

But Chanla's heart wasn't in this place, not yet. Every day his mind filled with thoughts of his wife and baby, and he prayed fervently for their safety. He felt guilty for leaving them behind. He wouldn't be able to forgive himself if anything happened to them.

In about ten days, he received a note:

> We are fine. Mother is still stubborn about leaving.
> I will wait two more weeks.
> Vandy

That afternoon he passed a building where people were singing. Gospel hymns! He hadn't heard songs like that for more than five years. He went to the door, and a friendly couple welcomed him inside. He sat down, and someone handed him a Bible.

A Bible! A *whole* Bible in his hands once more! He opened it lovingly. With joy he began reading the familiar words in his own language.

At the end of the meeting, he asked the man if it was possible to get a Bible for himself. "Take this one," he said.

Hardly believing his ears, Chanla looked up to see if the man really meant it. He was smiling. "Take it home and study it. Come back next Sunday at 4:00 p.m., and we'll have another meeting."

The following week, Chanla brought the whole family.

The group was studying the book of Matthew, and Panno requested a Bible of his own. He was so excited about having something to read that he spent hours studying it. He was also anxious to find out more about Chanla's God, a God he himself was learning to trust.

Each morning, Chanla faithfully went to the entrance of the camp, and then to the processing center to see if Vandy had come. One morning he heard her familiar voice: "Chanla, we are here! Your wife and son."

As Chanla hugged them, Vandy continued, "Mother wouldn't come. She said she and her sister decided they were too old to start a new life. They want to live and die in their own country, no matter how bad things get. She finally told me to go."

"Maybe that's best for them, dear one," Chanla said gently. "But we are young. We have our whole lives ahead of us."

He picked up the baby and put his other arm around Vandy Kim. "Come and see our new home."

Their quest was almost over.

Chapter 18
True Freedom

As Chanla cleared a space on the shelf for Vandy's things, he noticed the neat pile of Father's clothes.

"Look at this," he exclaimed. "Do you suppose Mother still clings to the possibility that Father has survived?"

Pitura sat nearby holding the baby. "Perhaps," she said thoughtfully, "but I believe it's more than that. Having a few of Father's things gives her a feeling of 'connectedness.' She hasn't lost all of him, because she can still touch things he touched, still hold things he loved close to her heart."

"I'm sure you're right, Pitura. Her devotion to Father's memory is as strong as the love they shared." Chanla's eyes misted as he looked at his own wife. He thanked God they had both survived.

Chanla took Vandy around the camp, introducing her to their new friends and their new life. As Chanla spoke freely about the things on his mind, Vandy felt uneasy and began glancing about. Before, they had only whispered of such things. Just one careless remark could cost a person's life!

Chanla noticed her nervousness and laughed at himself. "I'm getting more accustomed to freedom than I realized! It's so different here. You can say what you want."

That night, Chanla picked up his Bible and turned to his wife. "Sweet one, remember I told you how Mother risked her life to save my little half-Bible while I was in prison? And remember how much I missed it after we left Nong Chan Camp? Well, I now have another one, a whole Bible this time." He placed it in Vandy's hands. She was a bit startled, but finally opened it.

"It looks like it's printed in our own language," she said with a touch of awe. She looked up at her husband, realizing how much this meant to him. "Will you teach me to read it? I've always wanted to learn to read."

Chanla squeezed her hand. "You surely will learn to read this wonderful Book. And I have another surprise. Every Sunday a group of friendly people meet to study this Bible. I'll take you with us next time."

As the lessons proceeded through the book of Matthew, Chanla watched his family. Mother, Panno, Pitura, and Piteak were openly enthusiastic, though Piteak admitted his main motivation was to learn English.

"I've been so intent on surviving, on caring for the family, that I've given little thought to spiritual things," he explained. "But I admire you and your faith, and I'm willing to learn about it."

Grandma was openly worried. Chanla could imagine how she felt, having spent a lifetime in a culture that heavily embraced the Buddhist philosophy. Could someone eighty years old make an about-face in attitudes and beliefs?

"You are a good boy," she told Chanla, patting his cheek. "I will come and find out for myself what these people are teaching."

The smaller children already loved Chanla's Bible stories and were attracted by this new Jesus, a Person who could feed 5,000 people with two small fish, who made sick people well, and who loved to hold children on His lap. They sat on the front row every week.

Only Vandy was silent. She listened and watched without comment. Chanla longed for his young wife to embrace his faith in God. Though they had been married for a year and a half, they'd spent little time together. Christianity was a new and strange concept to her.

During the early weeks, the thrill of freedom and their new life totally occupied them. Everything was different.

No longer did they live in fear and chronic hunger. Doors to knowledge began to crack open. People could walk about when they pleased, talk openly, and worship as they chose. The dignity of the individual was restored.

Besides the Cambodian peasants, the camp sheltered refugees from Laos and Vietnam, and even a few Khmer Rouge. Many relief agencies worked in the camps, among them the Red Cross, World Vision, UNESCO, and various church groups. These people also assisted the refugees in locating sponsorships to other countries.

Chanla and his family couldn't think of a single person they knew in another country. They puzzled and prayed about this. Other than risking a return to Cambodia, no other way existed to get out of the refugee camp.

In time, Chanla heard that an uncle, one of Father's older brothers, had reached the United States. He promptly wrote him a letter explaining their situation and requesting sponsorship for their family.

Then they waited and waited, keeping as busy and cheerful as possible. They reminded themselves that this was only a temporary period, until they could reach a new destination. Daily they looked for a letter, but each day they were disappointed. As the days dragged into weeks and the weeks into months, the dreariness of their situation pressed in on them. Chanla wrote Uncle again, and the waiting continued.

Chanla and Panno looked around for work. Chanla began teaching English classes, and Panno found a group of children that needed a teacher. The women cooked meals and watched the little ones.

As the months dragged on, time hung heavily on all of them. Although people could move about freely inside the camp, no one could leave unless a person from outside came for them and posted a guarantee. Being unable to speak the Thai language posed another barrier. Chanla met families who had spent years in camp, with diminishing hopes of getting out.

Chanla began to sense a new kind of oppression. They were virtually prisoners to a primitive life in an increasingly crowded camp. Boredom crept in and became a growing problem. The camp offered too much time, too little to do, and nowhere to go. Their bright dreams began to wither. They had suffered so long and survived so much! Was it to be for nothing? Would they slowly rot in this God-forsaken piece of nowhere?

The lack of activity and challenge took its toll on Grandma. The children grew listless. Pitura often cried herself to sleep. Piteak and Panno became irritable, roaming about camp and kicking at small sticks and rocks with unnatural fierceness.

Mother circulated around the camp determinedly cheerful, making new friends and gathering tidbits of news to share with the family. But their increasing depression worried her, and her own pillow was often wet.

Five months went by, and life for the Dok family reached a new low. No word came from Uncle, and with no relief in sight, time seemed to stretch into infinity.

Chanla's own faith was sorely tested. To fight his discouragement, he turned increasingly to his Bible. Reading the story of Joseph, he pondered the young man's cheerfulness and faithfulness during long years of undeserved confinement. Joseph trusted his God.

Chanla turned to the New Testament and read from Paul's writings. This strong, active man was not defeated by imprisonment either. He continued writing letters of encouragement, and he spoke cheerfully to everyone he saw. His words, "I have learned to be content whatever the circumstances" (Philippians 4:11, NIV), became a motto for Chanla.

With his own faith refreshed, Chanla called the family together. Little Rith crawled to his father and fastened himself onto one of Chanla's legs. From this secure vantage point, he looked around happily at the others. Smiles began to appear on faces around him. "We couldn't have had a better demonstration of what I want to tell you tonight," Chanla began. "The last few weeks have been most trying for all of us. We are rested, refreshed, and ready to get on with our lives, yet we sit here day after day, like animals in a cage. Right now, we can't see any way out. We've been unable to reach our uncle, and we don't know of anyone else who can help us.

"But these past few weeks, we have also been studying about the great God in heaven. He loves us with a greater love than it's possible for me to love my little son." He picked up Rith and hugged him.

"As you know, I put my life in this God's hands six years ago. He has been with me, comforted me, and given me strength in every conceivable situation since that time. He is caring for us right now. He will not let us perish in this place.

"Remember the story of Daniel. He was taken captive while still in his teens and carried off to a strange land. The king even decreed his death. But Daniel completely trusted his God, and in time he was able to fill an important place in the government of Babylon. In the end, the Lord used him mightily to bring the knowledge of the true God to many kings and nations."

Everyone listened, and Chanla continued. "And remember poor Jonah. He felt he couldn't face the job God asked him to do. If anyone was ever depressed, it was this man. In desperation, during a storm, he begged his friends to throw him overboard from the ship and end his life quickly. He felt as low and as near death as a human can get. But God knew where he was and rescued him in a very unique way. Jonah became a mighty prophet and one of the authors of the Bible.

"Dear family," Chanla concluded, "this same God is still alive. We have experienced His special care and protection for several years. He won't forget us now.

"When we feel discouraged, let's think about Daniel and about Jonah. And about Ruth, the Moabite woman," he added, looking at Pitura.

"I feel that God is very near to us, even in this seemingly forgotten camp. We are alive and well. I believe we will yet have an opportunity to be of useful service. We need to trust the great God above as my little Rith trusts his earthly father."

It was a long speech for the usually quiet Chanla. But the strength of his faith glistened like a bright jewel on the gray landscape of their present life. Chanla hugged the children. Mother's eyes were wet.

Panno stood up, snapped his fingers, and yelled, "*Daniel!*" He winked at Chanla.

Not to be outdone, Piteak followed suit, shouting, "*Jonah!*"

On her way to bed that night, Pitura detoured toward Chanla with a glint in her eyes. "*Ruth!*" she whispered as she passed him.

The good humor persisted in the days that followed. It became a game of sorts. If Piteak looked too serious, Mother would cuff him playfully, saying, "*Daniel!*" One day, Grandma, seeing Chanla puzzling over a piece of broken equipment, looked at him and said, "*Jono!*" She mangled the name, but caught the spirit. Chanla sat back and laughed. What a dear, precious family!

As family morale improved, Mother felt better. She lay on her mat at night thinking about the family's good fortune. They were together. They had shelter and food. Torture and death no longer haunted them. Though Father was lost to them, Chanla and Panno, barely eighteen and seventeen at the beginning of their ordeal, had persevered, caring for and protecting them throughout the years. Chanla, especially, had inspired courage and strength in each of them during times when life seemed hopeless. Mother began formulating a plan.

The following evening she called the family together. As they gathered in a somewhat jagged circle, little Rith gleefully went from one to the other, receiving hugs and pats, handing each one a toy, then returning to reclaim it. Chanla thanked God again for this little sunbeam. Caring for the active, happy little boy had also kept Vandy busy and cheerful.

Mother had a small package in her hand. "This is the most precious possession I have from our past life," she began, unwrapping the object and displaying a beautiful and valuable old ring.

"This heirloom has been passed from one generation to the other," she explained. The family had seen this ring a long time ago, but had no idea it had been preserved.

Mother turned to Chanla, her eyes glowing with pride

and love. "My son, I cannot express in words what you have meant to me and to our whole family these past five years. Although we lost Father, you have filled his shoes very well. You have cared for us, encouraged us, and prayed for us. Your strong faith in your God has inspired us when we felt tempted to give up."

Mother paused, lips quivering. She regained control and continued. "According to Cambodian custom, sons are nourished and sheltered in their homes until they marry. You are now married and have a son of your own. You are also the firstborn son, the head of the family. It is time to pass to you this heirloom, this symbol of your leadership and of the continuity of the family."

Deeply touched, Chanla knelt before his mother. As he accepted the ring, he looked into her face. How he loved this extraordinary woman! Deep in his heart he knew that whatever strength he had shown during the past six years had been more than equaled by her own.

But Mother wasn't finished yet. "I have another son," she continued, turning to Panno, "who, alongside his brother, has gallantly done his part to fill Father's shoes." She smiled her special little smile again.

"Panno came face to face with death and willed himself to live until he could reach his home and family. But his life was spared. A few weeks ago, with wisdom and care beyond his years, he arranged a safe trip for us to freedom."

Mother smiled again and held up another package. "I have a gift for you also. It may not have monetary value, but it is priceless. I want you to have Father's watch."

Panno, who was seldom serious about anything, felt tears coming. Father's watch. What a treasure! He, too, knelt before his mother and accepted the gift with deep emotion.

The night's experience warmed the whole family, and they felt a renewed pride in their kinship.

A few days later, Panno, always restless, always the first one up each morning, went to headquarters looking for news. And there, on the bulletin board, *were the names of his family!*

Within minutes, his excited shouts woke everyone. "Our names have been posted! We are to be transferred to the Chonburi Transit Center."

"That means Uncle must have answered our plea. He is sponsoring us!" Chanla's excitement matched his brother's.

Within minutes the whole family trooped over to see for themselves. There it was: THE DOK SAVANG FAMILY— REPORT FOR IMMEDIATE TRANSFER TO CHONBURI CAMP.

It didn't take long to get ready. Carrying their belongings in boxes and bags, they bade their friends goodbye and boarded the bus for Chonburi.

Life at the Chonburi Transit Center was a great improvement. No robbers patrolled about outside the camp, preying on restless refugees who might climb the fence for an excursion into the forest. The food was good, and their quarters were even better.

An entirely different spirit was present there. The people had sponsors and were preparing themselves for their future homes. Sponsoring countries included England, Australia, Canada, France, and the United States. Families were assigned to orientation classes specific to the language and culture of the places to which they were going.

Chanla again found himself in demand as an English teacher, and Panno worked as a counselor for refugee problems. Panno also taught part time at a Cambodian preschool. During the week their many activities kept the family busy and challenged.

By week's end, Panno and Chanla decided to look for a new Bible study group. They noticed people gathering on a large porch of the CARE building.

"What's the attraction?" they asked a young man headed that way.

"Some American missionaries come here each week to teach the Bible. The classes are very interesting. Why don't you come this morning and see for yourselves?"

The man's enthusiasm sparked their curiosity. A jeep pulled up, and the missionaries and their friends disembarked. Chanla and Panno were introduced and welcomed. The people divided into smaller groups, and classes were conducted all morning. Chanla and Panno were invited back in the afternoon.

"We must bring our Bibles," Chanla said. "They check to see what the Bible says on every point they talk about. That's the most interesting class I've ever attended."

"I like the way we can all pitch into the discussions," Panno replied. "I learned a lot today."

The rest of the family accompanied the brothers to the afternoon meeting. The program was more casual, and the missionaries spent time getting acquainted with the Dok family. As soon as they discovered Chanla's Christian background, they asked him to lead one of the study groups. Panno showed a good grasp of Christian principles as well and by the second week was put in charge of another discussion group.

In the following weeks, the family learned about God's creation and original plans for the earth, the beginning of sin, and the ensuing battle between good and evil. They finally began to understand the meaning of the cruelty and suffering they'd experienced.

As they studied the life of Jesus Christ, the lessons became even more real to them. Jesus left heaven and came down to earth as a baby. He grew into manhood living with the people of His time, sharing their joys and sorrows. He touched lepers, healed the lame, and fed the hungry. In the end, He was betrayed by an associate, deserted by His friends, tortured and killed in a cruel and heartless manner. The refugees understood these experiences. They were deeply touched to learn there was a God in heaven who cared about them personally, to whom their lives actually mattered.

Panno was the first to request baptism. "I have watched my brother live as a Christian under the most difficult possible circumstances," he told the missionaries. "It was due to his strong faith and prayers to God and the devoted love and care of my mother that I am alive today. I have been privately praying to Chanla's God for several years, though I was not sure just who He was. Now that I know Him for myself, I want to give my life to Him."

Pitura was next. "I, too, have been praying to Chanla's God," she explained. "I have seen with my own eyes how this God has comforted and strengthened my brother when the rest of us gave up hope. I, too, desire to become a Christian and belong to the family of Jesus."

Piteak was surprised at himself. He had taken the Bible lessons simply to learn English, not feeling any spiritual inclinations. But as the studies progressed, his attitude changed. He began to grasp the larger plan that God had for humanity, a plan that far surpassed anything he had ever dreamed. He became excited over the knowledge that an eternal plan existed for his own life. Other interests paled by comparison.

Grandma worried over the turn of events. Even though she loved Chanla and admired his Christian principles, she still could not feel comfortable with a new God. Because she had never heard of Him during most of her life, she felt He must be a foreigner's God. She wasn't sure He fit into the Cambodian way of life. Now that the family was leaving their homeland, she determined that she must continue to keep the old traditions alive.

"Grandson, I love you and will not oppose you. You are a fine man." Grandma sighed deeply. "Maybe I'm too old, but I'm fearful of change. For years, even before the Khmer Rouge took over, I've watched young people grow more and more careless of spiritual things. They act like our temples are places for social gatherings, rather than worship. Our country has a strong spiritual heritage, and I feel I must remain loyal to what I know. I hope you will understand and accept my decision."

Chanla held his dear little grandma close. He realized how much like her the whole family was proving to be: open, honest, independent, each determined to follow individual convictions.

Mother was caught in-between. She believed in Chanla's God and had long been praying to Him. She confessed to Chanla that she had lost her confidence in the Buddhist faith during their time as refugees in Vietnam. "I saw that our gods had no interest in us. They offered no real hope. We were alone in the universe, waiting to die, hoping to gain a better spot in the next life, of which we could never be sure. It depressed me so much that I began asking your God to look after us."

Chanla was amazed. His mother already had a budding Christian experience.

"However, I have great respect for Grandma. I don't want to upset her during these crucial days ahead. When the others are baptized, I will be praying to God to accept me as I am. He knows my heart, and my heart is a Christian heart. In time, I'll be able to join the church in a more complete way."

Vandy sought out her husband privately. "Dear husband, I know you are praying for me. I also want to share the Christian way." She hesitated, shy, yet determined. "But it is still very new to me. There is much I don't yet understand. The baby keeps me distracted from the lessons. Be patient with me. I'll continue to study, and when I am ready, I'll become a Christian with my full heart."

Chanla loved this open, forthright girl more than ever before. The oriental custom was for women to submit themselves to their husband's will, but Vandy would have none of it. She sought the truth with sincerity and would be true to her own conscience.

Uncertainties still loomed ahead and sometimes nearly overwhelmed them. How would they get to America? Would they be accepted? Would they be able to adapt to such completely different customs, language, ways of living and thinking? Could they survive in such a different world? Maybe they would die of homesickness!

But as their faith in God and love for Jesus Christ grew, their doubts and fears began to shrink and gradually disappear. Soon, nothing could dampen their growing enthusiasm. They were finally discovering the one true freedom, the freedom of mind, soul, and spirit that no earthly power could destroy. They stopped fearing the future. Even separation and death lost their terror. In God's family they would be safe for eternity.

December 6, 1980, was the happiest day of Chanla's life. He remembered the words he had read so long before—words St. Paul had written in prison:

"I know that this will turn out for my salvation through your prayer and the supply of the Spirit of Jesus Christ" (Philippians 1:19, NKJV).

He remembered his own prayer that day, asking God to use the experiences they were going through to bring salvation to his family as well as to himself.

Standing beside the river that morning, Chanla's prayers were answered and his dreams realized as Panno, Pitura, and Piteak were baptized. The younger children hugged the Bible and told the missionaries that when they were old enough, they, too would be baptized. Mother, standing on Chanla's right, reached up and squeezed his arm, indicating her personal dedication. Vandy, on his left, leaned toward him and whispered, "This is such a beautiful experience! My heart is with you." Grandma got caught up in the joy of the day and began hugging all the "new Christians."

Five and a half years after their lives were shattered by a ruthless, godless regime, the Dok family was freed for eternity by accepting Jesus Christ. Now, the Man from Galilee, who had conquered death and pain for all time, was their Guide and their Leader.

Their quest for freedom was over. No power on earth could force their steadfast allegiance from the great Giver of hope!

Epilogue

The Dok family arrived in the United States on September 18, 1981. The succeeding years have brought many changes.

At this writing, Prok, Vivatny, and Chande have been baptized and are active church members. Prok is now a university student studying architecture. Vivatny, now in college, wants to take dentistry. Chande, a straight-A student, dreams of becoming a physician.

After a slow start, Piteak grew to be the tallest brother. He is completing studies toward a degree in electrical engineering and works for a chemical company.

Skinny little Pitura is now a stunning young woman, her beautiful hair once again gracing her shoulders. A serious-minded university student, she is pursuing a degree in computer science. She recently married a fellow Cambodian Christian who was also once a refugee, and they have a baby son.

Panno now works with an employment agency that specializes in finding jobs for new immigrants. Along the way, he fell in love with a young secretary in his church. They've set up their own home and are rearing two little sons.

Grandma retained her active mind and interest in life until the end. She made sure that none of the little ones grew up without a knowledge of their Cambodian culture and roots; and that the older ones didn't forget. She died peacefully last year at age 89.

Mother continues to cherish the little pile of Father's clothes, which remain stacked near her own. Her natural entrepreneurial instincts have paid off in the form of a thriving local diamond-appraisal business. But her main interest continues to be caring for her loved ones. Except for Panno and Chanla, the rest of the family still live at home.

Vandy's mother resisted all efforts to rescue her from the Cambodian refugee camp. Vandy and Chanla faithfully sent her money, food and medicines, until they were informed of her death in 1989.

Looking at Chanla today, strong and healthy, with his kind eyes, gentle manners, and ready smile, it's hard to realize that this is the same young man who lived through the events in this story. He and Vandy share a growing Christian faith as well as a maturing Christian marriage. Sixth-grader Rith, totally Americanized, has been joined by two younger brothers: Daniel and Jonah!

Chanla is completing university studies toward a degree in religion and ministerial studies this summer. He edits a quarterly newsletter for an international Cambodian Christian group. He is preparing a series of weekly Christian radio programs to be broadcast into his homeland. He and Panno also translate Bible lessons and other Christian literature into the Cambodian language, using a special word processor.

On weekends, Chanla serves as lay pastor for a growing flock of Cambodian Christians. The entire family now worships in their little church.

Chanla was delighted recently to hear from his old friend Pran, who is also in the States.

Life continues to be a challenge for Chanla. Juggling jobs, schoolwork, church duties, and family responsibilities with all the other demands of modern American life, he faces the same problems as the rest of us, and the same frustrations.

"You know," he observed recently, reflecting on his experiences, "during all those years of hardship and persecution, I never had a headache. But in my life today, I have a headache nearly every week!"

The horrors are gone, but the past cannot be forgotten. Nightmares occasionally persist. The family prays daily for their suffering "brothers and sisters" who are still in Cambodia and in the refugee camps. Psalm 91 has become a special passage of comfort to the family.

"I will say of the Lord, 'He is my refuge and my fortress; my God, in Him will I trust' " (Psalm 91:2, NKJV).

When
the
storms
of life
rage,
you need
more than
an umbrella.

**You need
shelter.**

Glib answers and worn-out clichés about the meaning of suffering are about as effective as an umbrella in a hurricane.

Pain, disappointment, and grief are real. And they hurt.

From a man who knows what it means to walk through "the valley of the shadow of death," comes a brilliant, sensitive survival guide for believers who are hurting and struggling to face another day.

Jeris Bragan's *When You Walk Through a Storm* deals both with the down side of life and the reality of God's healing presence for those who hurt.

If you need shelter from the storm, this is it.

US$7.95/Cdn$9.95
Paper, 128 pgs.

Please photocopy and complete order form below.

YOU WON'T BELIEVE IT. BUT YOU MUST.